STAT FREE SIX SIGMA

Focusing on Intent for Quick Results

Praveen Gupta, Six Sigma Master Black Belt,
Arvin Sri, Six Sigma Black Belt
ACCELPER CONSULTING
<u>www.accelper.com</u>

Please contact us to buy multiple copies of this book, or to receive volume discount. For more information, contact:

Accelper Consulting
1320 Tower Road
Schaumburg, IL 60173

Tel: (847) 884-1900
Fax: (847) 884-7280
E-mail: info@accelper.com

Publisher   - BookSurge, LLC
                       An Amazon.com Company
                     - Accelper Consulting
Editor   - Shellie Tate
Cover Design   - Dan Pongetti

Stock printing and binding by Thomson-Shore, Inc., Dexter, MI. United States of America

ISBN # 1-4196-5458-6
Library of Congress Control Number: 2007900172

The authors would like to dedicate this book to parents, grandparents and their friends for their continual emphasis on education and excellence in everything.

Especially attributed to Arvin's Daadi.

About the Authors

Praveen Gupta, President of Accelper Consulting, has been working in the business performance improvement field since 1980. He worked at Motorola in the Semiconductor Product Sector and Communications Sector and at AT&T Bell Laboratories for nine years. He founded Accelper Consulting (formerly Quality Technology Company) in 1989 to provide training and consulting services to businesses. Accelper Consulting is focused on improving business performance through quality methods as well as developing new tools when needed.

Praveen has been working on Six Sigma since its inception and has recently looked beyond Six Sigma as well as at challenges in improving performance. As a result of his experience with more than 100 companies, he has developed a Strategy for Execution Map that consists of five items, namely:

1. Rapid Benchmarking for setting goals
2. Six Sigma Business Scorecard for monitoring performance
3. Six Sigma for improving profit
4. Business Innovation for achieving growth
5. The 4P (Prepare, Perform, Perfect, and Progress) Model for sustaining process excellence

Praveen has trained executives for Motorola University in Six Sigma, Design for Manufacturability, Cycle Time Reduction, Statistical Process Control and Managing Continuous Improvement. He has consulted with more than one hundred corporations in achieving improved performance.

Praveen holds an MSEE in Electrical and Computer Engineering from the Illinois Institute of Technology, Chicago, and is a CQE, a CSQE and a PE in Illinois. He is also an ASQ Fellow and a Six Sigma Master Black Belt. Praveen has published several books, including his best-selling *Six Sigma Business Scorecard, The Six Sigma Performance Handbook, Business Innovation,* and *Improving Quality in Healthcare.*

Praveen can be contacted at Accelper Consulting at (847) 884-1900 or by email at praveen@accelper.com.

Arvin Sri, a Senior Consultant at Accelper Consulting, has over 20 years of experience in business process improvement and Six Sigma in several industries. Arvin has helped Accelper's clients by providing Six Sigma Green Belt training and assisting clients through guiding Six Sigma projects successfully. His process approach helps clients achieve benefits with short-term deadlines. He helps clients implement enterprise-wide management systems to sustain improved processes.

Prior to joining Accelper Consulting, Arvin worked for ICI and Siemens. He led the teams for process improvement and cost-saving projects in the areas of sales, planning, purchasing, inventory management, distribution and outsourcing.

Arvin is a contributing author to *The Six Sigma Performance Handbook* and *Six Sigma for Transactions and Service*, both published by McGraw-Hill. Arvin works with Praveen on several research projects.

Arvin's areas of interest include customer relationship management, teamwork, project leadership, communication, process thinking, statistical thinking, and performance improvement. Arvin holds a BSME from IIT Roorkee, an MSIE from NITIE Mumbai, and an MBA from Benedictine University, Illinois.

Table of Contents

Foreword

When people hear the term Six Sigma, they perceive it to be a series of complex formulas and statistics. Once they understand that Six Sigma really has two components — a statistical term meaning a 3.4-defects-per-million defect rate, and, more importantly, a methodology for improving business processes — then they recognize its value. It is this latter component that is the focus of most Six Sigma initiatives.

As Vice President of Quality at Motorola when Six Sigma spread rapidly throughout our corporation, I witnessed dramatic improvements in operational performance. I recognized that the most significant improvements resulted from the use of simple tools and measurements and by following the philosophy of continual improvement – whether in a manufacturing, marketing, sales, or human resources capacity. We learned quickly that the keys to successful implementation of any Six Sigma initiative were a common foundational skill set and support from all levels of management.

Despite the many Six Sigma tools available for use, it is the "stat free" Six Sigma tools that generate the biggest improvements. I often have the opportunity to meet people currently involved in Six Sigma initiatives in many industries — nonprofit, finance, and manufacturing, among others. When I probe for the tools used most frequently, they cite "Stat Free" Six Sigma tools, such as Process Mapping, Pareto, and Root Cause Analysis.

In this book, the authors succeed in explaining the basics of Six Sigma, the required Six Sigma skills, and how to implement a successful Six Sigma initiative. They provide the reader with a foundational set of "Stat Free" Six Sigma tools that can be applied to each phase of the Six Sigma DMAIC problem-solving methodology. The authors emphasize the importance of innovation and demonstrate to the reader how to use innovation when implementing Six Sigma projects in today's competitive global business environment.

Perhaps the title of this book has two meanings: "Stat Free" referring to the non-statistical aspect of Six Sigma; but also the more subtle "static free" way to learn Six Sigma!

Gayle Landuyt
Director of the Management Development Center
DePaul University
Chicago, Illinois
December 20, 2006

Acknowledgements

We would like to acknowledge our clients, colleagues, friends, and students for their continual input about challenges with implementing Six Sigma as well as the demand for practical solutions.

We would like to express our gratitude to our families (Nidhi, Anubhav, Archana, Krishna, and Avanti) for their support for our writing binge to complete this book with a sense of urgency around Christmas. This support has been a lot to ask for around the holidays.

Finally, we would like to acknowledge prompt help from Dan Pongetti, Shellie Tate, and Roy Francia throughout the publishing process. We would also like to acknowledge the following organizations or publications for their support to authors' prior work:

McGraw-Hill
Quality Digest
Circuits Assembly
PC FAB Magazine
UP Media Group
QSU Publishing Company
Scanlon Leadership Network

Finally, we would like to thank you, the reader, for supporting the practical approach to implementing Six Sigma.

Praveen Gupta
Arvin Sri

Preface

With maturity of the Six Sigma methodology, companies expect to implement Six Sigma cost effectively without its esoteric complexities. Six Sigma was developed as a means to accelerate improvement – not to become the end in itself. Thus Six Sigma must become an easily understandable and usable methodology in order to maximize its benefits. Otherwise, the old paradigm of 'Program of the Year' will prevail, and somebody will name it something else, impose it on their suppliers, and perpetuate waste of precious business resources.

We recognize that we, as consultants, do our fair share and take the next bold step of right-sizing the role of statistics in the success of Six Sigma. We understand readers' discomfort with the statistical aspects of Six Sigma and thus have simplified them. We have not eliminated the statistics entirely, but we have come close to virtually eliminating statistics out of Six Sigma. We have first highlighted the non-statistical tools, which are more valuable than statistical tools, and then we have simplified the statistical tools. In so doing, people can now focus more on the application of these tools, and thus the practice of statistical thinking.

Rote application of any tool without the right thinking, as well as failure to understand its intent, will lead to frustration due to lack of results. Through simplification of statistics and selection of key tools, we hope readers will have more time to think and creatively apply the methodology and tools, thus maximizing the benefits of Six Sigma.

Thinking of Six Sigma...

The purpose of a business is not to make money;
instead it is to provide value to the customer.

If the job is done well in providing the value,
the business makes money.

To do well means achieving excellence,
which does not imply 'zero' defects.

Excellence is all about achieving perfection,
which is not to stay within arbitrary limits.

Perfection means being on target, and excellence implies
reducing inconsistencies around the target.

Target is defined by the customer,
and limits are guided by economics.

We must produce on target and deliver within limits.

Customers like minimal inconsistencies around the target;
Six Sigma is designed to reduce inconsistencies.

Six Sigma is an approach to achieve excellence fast
by understanding the cause and effect relationships.

- Praveen Gupta

CHAPTER ONE

INTRODUCTION

Reminiscing on my early days of Six Sigma when my boss said, "Three Sigma will not be enough," I thought one of my many bosses was very knowledgeable in statistics. He knew the language, and of course, I had never seen him using any of the statistical tools he talked about. Since the launch of Six Sigma in 1987, thousands of corporations have implemented it. Actually, Six Sigma became popular after its successful implementation by GE. Jack Welch became the spokesperson for Six Sigma, raising its profile to the board room and on Wall Street.

As a result of GE's success, the Six Sigma bandwagon started its journey, and many corporations, consultants, statisticians and aspirants have jumped in. Six Sigma has been redefined and standardized. The standardization of a routine methodology (which Six Sigma has become) is understood; losing some key aspects, however, as well as an overemphasis on statistics, has limited its benefits to users.

The problem of Six Sigma begins with the definition of Six Sigma. According to the definition of Six Sigma as captured on iSixSigma.com, a major discussion hub for Six Sigma professionals, *"Six Sigma is a disciplined, data-driven approach and methodology for eliminating defects (driving towards six standard deviations between the mean and the nearest specification limit) in any process -- from manufacturing to transactional and from product to service."*

1

According to the early documents at Motorola, where Six Sigma was first used, a much simpler definition is found:
  "Six Sigma is our Five Year Goal to approach the Standard of Zero Defects, and be best-in-class in EVERYTHING we do."

One can adapt the original definition used at Motorola as the following:

Six Sigma is an approach to achieve virtual perfection fast, and be the best-in-class in everything we do.

To develop or deliver a solution virtually error-free, it must be designed with key characteristics such that the process variation remains about half of the specified tolerance, and thus the process average stays closer to the target. In other words, we must find a way to establish process capability such that the ratio of expected to actual performance stays equal to or greater than two. Thus Six Sigma performance implies the following:

(Designed Tolerance/Process Range) ≥ 2

The statistical definition focuses on tactics and tools, while the original definition focuses on the intent and methodology of Six Sigma. The intent of Six Sigma is to achieve a significant improvement fast by using the commonsensical (rather than statistical) DMAIC (Define, Measure, Analyze, Improve, and Control) methodology. Even in the methodology, significant improvement is achieved through the rigorous application of the tools identified in the Define phase. The Define phase is non-statistical. Without the Define phase, the rest of the methodology is an exercise in futility.

One of the challenges in corporate improvement initiatives is to sustain improvement. Today, to sustain means maintaining improvement rather than the status quo. To sustain improvement, conventional statistical process control tools alone are not enough. Instead tools to manage process performance must be in place, such as the 4P model consisting of prepare, perform, perfect, and progress. In addition, active management reviews, where the senior leadership demands continual improvement at an aggressive rate; ensures synergy among departments and people through compensation; and provides rewards for breakthrough improvement, aggressive goal-setting, and constant communication with employees, must exist. Thus the Control phase consists of mostly non-statistical tools.

Even the most commonly-used tools in the Measure, Analysis and Improve phases happen to be non-statistical. Furthermore, the tools that are purely statistical are needed rarely and actually cannot be effectively applied without first applying the non-statistical tools.

Today people are questioning Six Sigma for trivial issues like 1.5 Sigma shift, its buzz, the similarity with other known tools and methods, the 3.4 parts per million, or even its name. Key aspects of Six Sigma are being overlooked, and instead the focus is on its trivial aspects. Instead of honing in on intent, methodology, tools and measurements all together, we are picking up pieces that may have limited application and spending time discussing them. Again we must ask this question: "Can we use any of the tools in the Six Sigma tool box to become the best in what we do?" Instead of looking for faults, we must focus on benefiting from the methodology, knowing that most of the tools existed before the Six Sigma methodology.

The main difference between the known tools/methodologies and Six Sigma is that Six Sigma requires focus on producing results in a short time. Achieving the improvement is more important than applying a specific tool for improvement.

In a presentation titled *The Motorola Story* authored by the inventor of Six Sigma, Bill Smith, the term Six Sigma is used scarcely. Instead, Smith emphasized Motorola's goals as follows:

- Improve 10 times by 1989 (starting in 1987)
- Improve 100 times by 1991
- Achieve Six Sigma capability by 1992

Six Sigma capability was a goal of achieving virtual perfection through rapid improvement (about 90% reduction in defects or related waste every two years). Six Sigma is not about statistics; it is all about improvement. Motorola's success with Six Sigma was led by the innovative leadership of Bob Galvin and George Fisher, its sound strategic planning, and product innovation. Six Sigma supported Motorola's strategic initiatives by focusing on perfect execution.

Six Sigma cannot remedy strategic blunders; instead it can help companies step up from marginal performance to superior performance by accelerating improvement. In an article entitled *The Rival Japan Respects* in *Business Week* (November 1989), three Motorola secrets highlighted in the article were strong R&D, built-in quality, and zealous service. According to George Fisher, Motorola's CEO, the company reduced its defect rate from 3000 PPM to 200 PPM in about five years.

In the article *Motorola University: When Training Becomes an Education* published in *Harvard Business Review* (August 1990), William Wiggenhorn, President of Motorola University, states,

> The mathematics of quality is difficult. ...At Motorola we have nevertheless tried to teach at least a basic version of the math to every employee and to extend the concept and terminology of industrial quality into every corner of the business – training, public relations, finance, security, even cooking.

For a company committed to Six Sigma, what counts is the institutionalization of concepts and benefits rather than the cost of training and statistics. Employees must become better in what they do by incorporating basic analytical tools rather than becoming the analysts. Interestingly, an analysis of the body of knowledge for the ASQ-certified Black Belt program shows that about 80% of the tools are non-statistical, while the remaining 20% are statistical. However, 80% of the debate revolves around 20% of the statistical tools. We must instead practice simple tools, which are mostly non-statistical, and thus reap 80% of the potential benefits of Six Sigma.

One of the common challenges corporations face is how to incorporate Six Sigma in both the manufacturing and non-manufacturing operations of the organization. Six Sigma, even though used by many service organizations, is often perceived to be solely a manufacturing-oriented methodology.

All businesses have common processes such as sales, purchasing, quality, management, engineering, design and operations. Each process within a business requires people, material or information, machines or tools, and methods or procedures. When examining each process for its activities, a little difference does exist. The role of some components may vary. In the service industry, for example, people play a more important part, while software is the most important component in technology. No two processes are alike when examining them in this way.

Thus we must recognize differences, follow the common methodology, and produce different results such as the product, the service, or the solutions. The Six Sigma methodology is therefore applicable to all industries; however, it must be applied in a creative and productive manner rather than in a rote and unproductive manner. The focus must be on the business performance objectives as well as on the return on investment.

Interestingly, one of the brochures published by Motorola after winning the first Malcolm Baldrige Award includes the following quote:

> While the company expresses this (quality) goal in the language of statistics…the ultimate goal is zero defects in everything we do…The strategy is to refocus all elements of Motorola's business on serving the customer.

The above statement supports the idea that we must make right decisions based on facts and knowledge of the business. Sometimes facts are not available, but such a situation does not mean we simply gather facts forever or defer the decision. Instead, a cross-functional team must be able to make a decision based on its collective knowledge. Data become facts, facts become information, information becomes knowledge, and knowledge becomes intelligence that is used to make decisions.

We must not become slaves to so-called 'facts' as taught by some in the name of Six Sigma. Instead, we must be cognizant of facts and let data do the talking. If data are not present, we must observe, listen, and use intelligence to make decisions. One objective should be to avoid collecting too much data, thus leading to analysis paralysis.

Having worked with the inventor, taught thousands of people, and been in practice over twenty years, we have come to the conclusion that we must utilize Six Sigma as a methodology to accelerate improvement, instead of as a futile exercise in statistics. Employees should become more informed decision makers, be committed to excellence in a most effective manner, and contribute to the bottom line. Six Sigma must aid in contributing to the bottom line. If it does not, statistical tools will not help. On the other hand, many 'Stat Free' tools can help in improving the bottom line, and that is the intent of Six Sigma.

SIX SIGMA BACKGROUND

The Six Sigma Breakthrough

In the mid-eighties, Motorola's leadership was envisioning 15 years ahead and recognized that survival would be impossible without significantly changing its way of doing business. Various benchmarking studies showed that manufacturing capability must be as good as that of digital watches. Examining the expected quality level in parts per million (PPMs), and utilizing his knowledge of various statistical methods, Bill Smith invented Six Sigma concepts. While some may argue about the existence of statistics and various tools prior to the discovery of Six Sigma, Six Sigma as a quality initiative was developed by Bill Smith.

One of the fundamental observations Smith established is that field failures are nothing but escaping internal failures. Even today, almost every company measures customer satisfaction and quality of products or services in terms of parts per million, which normally is a small number. The ongoing challenge is that the customer wants the defective parts per million to be even smaller. Corporations formulate task forces to go after the customer PPMs. Smith discovered that defective PPMs received by the customer cannot be reduced without significantly reducing the number of defects observed internally. Thus measuring the internal defect rate is very critical, and dramatically reducing this internal defect rate is even more critical.

According to Smith's study, for every defect found by the customer, 10 defects will be caught internally. In order to reduce the last defect found by the customer, the organization must eliminate the 10 defects found internally by improving process consistency as well as the product design.

Return on Investment

Initially, organizations train a large number of Black Belts and Green Belts, which leads to the need for creating large numbers of Six Sigma projects. In one conference on this subject, the reported number of projects at a company exceeded 15,000. Such a situation leads to Six Sigma overhead to manage projects, monitor improvement, and ensure savings. Implementing project management software to handle this need can lead to some bureaucracy.

The challenge here is to ensure projects work out and show improvement. Due to a focus on project management, however, we lose focus on the project performance. Given the large number of projects, project performance becomes less visible, and consequently the manipulation begins. The improvement numbers are inflated and fabricated. This causes a challenge in correlating savings to Six Sigma projects. Establishing the savings from projects is then difficult due to the focus on project management rather than on project performance.

In the present evolution of Six Sigma, these issues are addressed. Corporations are implementing checks and balances to ensure credibility of cost savings based on Six Sigma and that savings links to corporate profitability.

Eventually, a significant return on investment for any Six Sigma initiative must be established.

Some of the factors corporations must address in order to capture savings may include the following:

- Opportunity cost or cost avoidance
- Savings schedule
- Unexpected adversaries erasing savings
- Investment in Six Sigma
- Gain sharing
- Accounting practices
- Financial reporting

To launch a Six Sigma initiative, profit-stream mapping must be performed, and various diversions or leakages of profit must be identified. Such analysis is a starting point for seeking leadership commitment as well as for setting expectations for savings and recognizing measurements for bottom-line impact. Six Sigma must eventually become a way of thinking and working — not an expensive add-on to existing systems.

In a recent implementation of Six Sigma at a small company, a few opportunities were identified and addressed. The company identified a corporate-level measurement system using the Six Sigma business scorecard framework and then drove its Six Sigma initiative by monitoring its corporate Sigma level. Like many companies, it did not commit a large amount of money to Six Sigma training. Instead, the company committed necessary resources to realize planned savings. The company leadership believes Six Sigma improved its bottom line by three to five percent in sales.

This percentage represents a significant and measurable improvement.

Justification for Six Sigma

Before we focus on savings, a company must establish right measurements for tracking progress of the Six Sigma initiative companywide — in other words the Sigma level for the corporation. The Sigma level highlights both strengths and weaknesses of a Six Sigma initiative. If a company's overall Sigma level is improving, the bottom line is bound to be affected positively.

With sound process management and corporate performance systems, tracking progress and savings becomes a natural byproduct of Six Sigma implementation. Six Sigma causes a significant improvement by doing things differently. If a few significant improvements are realized quickly, savings will be visible with the existing accounting system, which is less expensive than implementing a specific measurement system. If a lot of money must be spent in order to find out how much money has been made, we have lost Six Sigma.

Many executives wonder whether their company should commit to Six Sigma or not. To determine the potential benefits of Six Sigma, management must first understand the cost breakdown of its operations. The cost of providing service or producing product must be considered based on industry benchmarks. The cost of poor quality in terms of internal and external failures, as well as the cost of inspection, test or verification, must be reviewed. The cost of quality must be evaluated with respect to the profitability of the company instead of with respect to sales. Unless the facts about the company's performance are known, all initiatives will appear questionable.

For management to commit to launching a Six Sigma initiative, questions that must be answered include:
- What can Six Sigma do for my company in both the short and long term?
- How much will it cost?

Table 2.1 shows a simple analysis of Six Sigma implementation.

Table 2.1: Analysis of Six Sigma Implementation

Number of employees	100	1000
Annual sales (millions)	10	100
External Cost of implementing Six Sigma (millions)	0.25	1.0
Cost of poor quality at 20% (millions)	2	20
Minimum number of projects to be identified for breakeven	3	8
Minimum number of projects to be identified for 100% return on investment.	6	16
Number of Black Belts	1	5
Payback time after launch	1.5 yrs.	1.0 yr.

In this analysis, assumptions are made about the average project size, the sales, the number of employees to be trained as Six Sigma Green Belts or Black Belts, and the cost of poor quality in a company. Company-to-company variation should be expected; thus a company-specific analysis to determine the feasibility of the Six Sigma initiative should be performed.

Once the implementation of Six Sigma becomes an economically-viable strategy, management must consider giving its implementation the highest priority. Any competing initiative, conflicting priority or strategic initiative in progress must be clearly identified. Besides the economics, following is a list of critical success factors:

➢ passionate commitment to Six Sigma
➢ common language to be used throughout the organization
➢ aggressive improvement goals that will force continual process re-engineering
➢ innovation, not the statistics, as the key to achieving dramatic improvement
➢ process thinking for decision-making based on facts, and process knowledge
➢ correct metrics for assessing the next steps to achieve dramatic results
➢ improvement as a way of life; the company must plan to improve quality everyday
➢ employee engagement by making the Six Sigma initiative a rewarding experience
➢ communication to maintain continuity and interest in the Six Sigma initiative

The most critical success factor is the personal involvement of an organization's chief executive, which may inspire employees to do their best as they feel they are working for the chief executive. Employees are uplifted when they feel that they are involved in achieving a higher cause instead of simply performing daily duties.

Beyond the Fad

Six Sigma is a measure of the goodness of products and services. Higher Sigma means better quality of a product or service, and lower Sigma means poor quality of a product or service. The original Six Sigma initiative included leadership drive, the Six Steps methodology, and related measurements. The Six Steps are the following:

1. Define your products or services
2. Identify your customers and their critical needs
3. Identify your needs and resources
4. Map your process
5. Remove non-value-added activities and use error-free methods
6. Measure the Sigma level, and continue to improve the process if the Sigma level is less than 6.

Beyond the skepticism and challenges in implementing Six Sigma, today many small to large corporations have benefited from Six Sigma. The key aspects of successful implementation are aggressive goal-setting, graphical representation of performance against goals, effective management review, high executive management expectations, a standardized measurement system, and inspiring leadership.

Throwing dollars at Six Sigma alone will only accomplish waste. If Six Sigma is implemented correctly, organizations can see sales growth with higher profit margins. The perceived reputation, brand recognition, customer delight, and employee gain-sharing are some of the rewards of successful implementation.

Trouble with Six Sigma

After reviewing the implementation of Six Sigma at various companies, one of the most frequently occurring problems with Six Sigma is its use of statistics. Most employees do not like to become proficient statisticians. They do not mind using statistical thinking, facts-based decision-making, and even simple statistical tools, however. When employees see more complex tools, they tend to get nervous. This anxiety leads to employee resistance to Six Sigma.

A focus on measurements and tools trivializes the value, intent and methodology of Six Sigma. As a result, many Six Sigma implementations are perceived to be thoughtless actions or purposeless initiatives. Organizations attempt to implement Six Sigma, train their entire workforce, and still are unable to see any impact on the bottom line. Following is a list of main problems with Six Sigma:

1. Cannot generate savings
2. Rote application of the methodology
3. Too many trivial projects
4. Too much training
5. Expensive Six Sigma consulting
6. Too many statistics books converted into Six Sigma books, and too many consultants
7. Too much debate about Six Sigma and TQM
8. Treating Six Sigma like other programs of the year – yet another transient way to improve the bottom line
9. Local implementation without corporate commitment

10. Misunderstanding the intent of Six Sigma
11. Promoting the Check as learned in PDCA to achieve Six Sigma
12. Using processes without defined performance targets

Major positive changes from the successful implementation of Six Sigma include the following:

A. Focusing on the intent and the DMAIC methodology more than on tools and measurements
B. Understanding that excellence means perfection, and perfection means being on target
C. Designing processes and products with targets in mind

CHAPTER THREE

UNDERSTANDING
SIX SIGMA

For some, Six Sigma is a fact-based methodology made of fancy statistical tools that solve all business problems. For some, a misunderstanding exists between Six Sigma and karate because of the belts. For others, Six Sigma means DMAIC—Define, Measure, Analyze, Improve and Control.

Six Sigma was developed to become a best-in-class methodology by achieving virtual perfection in everything. It was a simple methodology that was rigorously implemented and passionately championed. It produced results, saving billions of dollars for many companies worldwide.

Effective Six Sigma means that its intent should first be understood before learning the methodology and tools. Statistical thinking is important in implementing Six Sigma well and is different from rigorous statistics. Statistical thinking means understanding the nature of variation, cause-and-effect relationships, and making adjustments accordingly.

One of the subtle aspects of a successful Six Sigma journey is driving out fear. Deming has emphasized driving out fear in bringing out the best in people. Employees are encouraged to take risks, learn from mistakes and accomplish breakthrough results. Six Sigma was used to achieve market leadership and the highest profit in the industry. Focusing on revenue growth concurrently with cost reduction will alleviate employees' fear of failure and of losing their jobs. Six Sigma means more capacity for growth, creating a positive environment and driving out fear.

Thus, one can define Six Sigma as a goal to achieve excellence and business objectives. It can be conceived as a strategy to immediately improve corporate profitability through waste reduction, achieve growth through sustained profits, and create a culture of continually achieving best-in-class performance through process reengineering.

Six Sigma can be thought of as having the following four elements:

1. Intent

The intent of Six Sigma is to achieve dramatic improvement quickly to become best-in-class in everything. If an organization wants to maximize return on investment in Six Sigma, it must institutionalize the expectation of dramatic improvement quickly. This expectation means everyone in the organization will set aggressive goals for improvement. Experience suggests that people have unlimited potential, and they will achieve what is expected of them. Employees will determine what they need to achieve dramatic improvement and ask for help as long as they know support is available.

In one company, the President said, "We have a good system, we achieve our goals, we have a consultant who guides us in setting our goals, and he ensures we meet our goals." Later he conceded that due to the pressure to meet goals, people set low expectations and thus produced marginal results. This company's profitability is about 3%. The profit is such that if one major problem develops, the profit will be wiped out, and the entire year will be wasted.

During ongoing discussion and after seeing higher profit, as well as an increase in his personal benefits, the President agreed to set higher expectations. One of the conditions to double the profit rapidly was to double employees' bonuses. As a result the net income was much more even after sharing the savings with employees. It made sense to the president, he announced doubling the employee bonus in five minutes, and this action got the ball rolling. After three months the company doubled its quarterly profit. Actually, the employee bonus quadrupled because of the doubling of the profit and the bonus rate. The President loved his share as well. He acknowledged that suddenly the profit gates had opened.

In another instance at a plant of a large corporation, the management team had set a low expectation for a newly-constructed factory. The low expectation meant 5% yield was considered to be good due to the complexity of the device and operations. When the goal is 5% yield, one can expect a variation around the average of 5% yield. Therefore, sometimes the yield may be zero, and sometimes it may be 8%. When the yield was 8%, the management took the credit and had a pizza party, but when the yield was 2%, it was attributed to the learning curve. The corporate management could not digest the 2-8% performance, as recovering investment in the plant appeared impossible.

The corporate management changed the leadership team at this plant. The entire team was fired. No low performers were tolerated – period. The new management team was implemented, it set a yield goal of 50% in six months, and it went after that goal. The plant achieved the 50% yield (or 900% improvement in six months). Employees enjoyed huge bonuses, bought new homes and new cars, or took expensive vacation trips.

Both companies achieved dramatic improvement quickly. Such is the intent of Six Sigma. After learning that projects drag on to an inconclusive ending, time is wasted in solving undefined problems, work is performed on conflicting projects due to a lack of planning, and proper documentation of accomplishment on the annual performance reviews is impossible, the need for Six Sigma becomes all the more apparent.

Prior to Six Sigma, organizations tried to implement TQM (total quality management), which promised results in about three years. Typically employees worked one year on TQM, its documents collected dust for another two years, and corporations waited for results forever (though of course, exceptions to this tendency of TQM do exist).

Therefore, Six Sigma was developed with the intent of accelerating improvement. Accelerating improvement means first creating a sense of urgency in what is accomplished, as well as expecting results in a short time. Due to this intent of Six Sigma, projects are defined and mapped out such that they can be completed and closed in four to six months. Furthermore, these projects must contribute to the bottom line. Depending upon the company size and burden cost, savings a project can range from $50,000 to $250,000.

The leadership has the responsibility to establish and communicate the intent of Six Sigma, which is dramatic improvement quickly. Here *dramatic* implies improvement significant enough to generate savings, and aggressive enough to demand employee creativity for reengineering the way of doing work. As long as a company achieves (or a project realizes) dramatic improvement quickly irrespective of the tools used for achieving the improvement, Six Sigma's intent is being fulfilled.

2. Six Sigma Methodology

When Six Sigma was implemented at Motorola in the late eighties, we worked off the intent and used whatever tools we were taught in our quality improvement training. We focused on six simple steps which highlighted knowing the customers, their critical needs, and our own needs first before measuring performance. Later, further successes led to the need for structuring and standardizing Six Sigma into some defined set of tools.

First MAIC was developed, and this evolved into DMAIC, where D stands for define, M stands for measure, A stands for analyze, I stands for improve, and C stands for control. Experience shows that D is the essential phase for achieving dramatic improvement quickly, and C is the most critical phase for realizing return on investment in Six Sigma projects. The Define phase requires the implementation of many tools, and the Control phase can aid in sustaining improved results, which requires the use of internal controls as well as management involvement.

The success of the DMAIC methodology depends on working well on the right projects. The right project is the one that has a significant return on investment. Sometimes people get training in Six Sigma but cannot find projects, or sometimes a company commits to Six Sigma but does not allow time to work on projects. Getting projects started is easy; the difficult part is completing and closing those projects.

Thus the first priority is to identify the right projects to work on which will have an impact on the bottom line and generate savings for the business. Several potential projects must be identified and evaluated based on a cost and benefit analysis. A simple measure, like the project prioritization index (PPI), can be used to prioritize projects according to the following equation:

$$PPI = (Benefits/cost) \times (Probability\ of\ Success/Time\ to\ complete\ the\ project\ in\ years)$$

At a minimum, the PPI should exceed 2 to ensure a return on investment. Initially one can find many projects with PPI greater than 4, thus making it somewhat easier to realize savings.

Once the project is selected, the team representing various functions is formed to work on it. The team receives the Six Sigma training at the Green Belt level while working on the selected project. During the Define phase, the team develops a clear definition of the project, the project's scope, the process map, customer requirements, SIPOC, and a project plan. In other words, in the Define phase, customer requirements are delineated and a process baseline is established.

In the Measure phase, we establish the sources of information, the performance baseline, and the opportunity's impact in terms of cost of quality. The performance baseline is established in terms of first pass yield (FPY), defects per unit (DPU), defects per million opportunities, Sigma level, and basic statistics such as mean and range or standard deviation.

In the Analyze phase, the focus is to examine patterns, trends, and correlations between the process output and its inputs. A cross-functional team performs the cause and effect analysis using the Fishbone diagram. The purpose is to identify the root cause of the problem and necessary remedial actions to capitalize the opportunity. At the end of the Analyze phase, the team is able to establish a relation such as $Y_{output} = f(x_{inputs})$.

While analyzing data, one should look into whether the excessive variation or inconsistency is normal in the process or has temporarily crept into the process. If the inconsistency is normal, a thorough capability study is required, and perhaps the process needs to be redesigned. If the inconsistency is exceptional, the process will need adjustment. Failure Mode and Effects Analysis (FMEA) is also used in the Analyze phase (or subsequent phases) to anticipate potential problems or risks, as well as to develop actions to reduce risks of failures.

The first three phases of the DMAIC methodology help in gaining a better understanding of the process and learning the cause-and-effect relationship between the output and input variables. The Improve phase enables the development of alternate solutions to achieve the desired process outcomes.

Typically in a non-Sigma environment, we jump to solving the problem directly without defining and understanding the process well. Without such an in-depth knowledge of the process, solving a problem becomes a game of luck.

Experimenting techniques are used to fine-tune the relationships or optimize the process recipe. However, such experiments are rarely required if non-statistical tools have been effectively utilized in the early phases.

The Control phase is employed to sustain the improvement utilizing effective documentation, training, process management, and process control techniques. In the Control phase, a score of the process or business performance must be maintained, and the Sigma level must be monitored. The Control phase is also an opportunity to engage the senior management in the Six Sigma journey for support and aggressive goal-setting.

One of the tools used in the Control phase is the 4P model, which is an improved version of the commonly-known PDCA. Here the 4Ps represent prepare, perform, perfect, and progress. Two main differences between the PDCA and 4P models are comprehensive preparation and the establishment of a performance target (rather then counting on Check to assess the performance). Six Sigma implies excellence, and excellence can only be achieved if the target is known.

3. Six Sigma Tools

The Six Sigma methodology incorporates numerous tools. The unique and useful Six Sigma tools include: Kano's model to capture customer critical requirements, SIPOC (Suppliers, Inputs, Process, Outputs, and Customers), Statistical software for analysis, Multi-vary analysis for identifying a predominant family of variation or inconsistencies, planned experimentation, and the 4P model to sustain gains. Table 3.1 summarizes simple yet powerful tools in the DMAIC methodology:

Table 3.1: Key DMAIC Tools

Phase	Tools
Define	Pareto, Process Map, Kano's Analysis, SIPOC, CTQ, Project Charter
Measure	Cost of Quality, DPU, DPMO, Sigma Level, Average, Range, Standard Deviation
Analyze	Root cause analysis, FMEA, Scatter Plot, Visual Correlation
Improve	Comparative and Full Factorial Experiments
Control (Sustain)	Process Thinking (4P model), Review, Control charts, Scorecard

While utilizing various Six Sigma tools, the dogma of statistics discourages many practitioners. In most cases in the manufacturing industry (as well as in the service and software areas), a lot of statistics need not to be used. Actually by utilizing some commonly-used tests for evaluating process improvement (using the mean or variance, for example), we have extracted the most likely statistics and presented them here in a simplified form.

4. Measurements

The three commonly-used measurements are DPU (defects/errors per unit), DPMO (defects per million opportunities), and Sigma level. The DPU is a unit or the output level measurement, DPMO is the process level measurement, and Sigma is a business level measurement. Sigma provides a common theme for the organization and requires a lot of improvement to show a positive change.

The customer cares for DPU, the process engineer needs to know DPMO, and the business needs to know the Sigma level. All of these measurements can be used to communicate performance expectations and progress throughout an organization.

The most commonly-used measurement driving improvement in an organization must be DPU. The DPU is converted into DPMO based on the process or product complexity, and the DPMO is transformed into the Sigma level for establishing a common performance measurement across all functions in an organization.

Executive Understanding of Six Sigma

The most critical factor in making a Six Sigma corporate initiative successful is the passionate commitment of leadership. However, passionate commitment must come with the correct understanding of the intent of Six Sigma and with effective executive support of the initiative. To create passionate commitment, leadership must learn certain tools and skills. These tools and skills are listed in Table 3.2.

Table 3.2 incorporates 10 tools an executive must become familiar with in order to actively participate in the Six Sigma initiative. With the help of these key executive tools, executives can steer their Six Sigma initiative in the right direction to achieve bottom line results. Otherwise, the Six Sigma implementation will staggeringly crash to the ground.

Table 3.2: Key Executive Tools for Six Sigma

Tool/Concept	When (Applicability)
Employee Recognition	To inspire dramatic improvement and employee innovation
Process Thinking	Helps understand business processes and how to lead them for improvement
Six Sigma Business Scorecard	Learning to achieve improvement in performance and profitability
Management Review	Monthly feedback to the management team for necessary adjustment to achieve growth and profitability
Statistical Thinking	Helps in determining degree of adjustment or type of actions to be taken
Six Sigma Overview	Decision making, specifically when committing to Six Sigma
Pareto Principle	When deciding about what to work on first
Process Mapping	Identifies disconnects in the business and opportunity for improvement
Cause and Effect Analysis	Identifies the root cause(s) of problems and remedial actions
Rate of Improvement	Achieves dramatic process improvement by reducing waste and achieving profitability

Six Sigma Thinking

As an organization makes the commitment to implement Six Sigma, one of the commonly-asked questions is about its effect on the corporate culture. People talk about cultural change, resistance to change, decision-making, and institutionalizing Six Sigma. Table 3.3 shows the extent of transformation needed at the thinking level in order for Six Sigma to become a way of doing work for achieving excellence and happy customers.

Table 3.3: Conventional vs. Six Sigma Thinking

ASPECT	CONVENTIONAL	SIX SIGMA THINKING
Management	Cost for Quality	Quality and Time
Manufacturability	Trial and Error	Robust Design
Variable Research	One-factor-at-a-time	Design of Experiments
Process Adjustment	Tweaking	Statistical Controls
Problem Solving	Expert Based	Process Based
Focus	Product	Process
Behavior	Reactive	Proactive
Suppliers Selection	Cost and Time	Process Capability
Decision Making	Intuition	Facts Based
Design	Creation	Reproducibility
Goal Setting	Realistic Perception	Reach out and Stretch
People	Cause of Problem	Asset and Solution
Improvement	Automation	Optimization

Ref: Harry and Schroeder, 2000

Six Sigma is a methodology, as well as a strategy, to achieve superior performance to become best-in-class in everything.

STAT-FREE SIX SIGMA TOOLS

The DMAIC methodology is a very important aspect of Six Sigma. An organization can benefit by institutionalizing DMAIC as a problem-solving approach; doing so will reduce the number of recurring problems. Just by following the DMAIC phases, improvement will be realized, because the problem will be better defined and the likely root cause will be identified. Six Sigma is about practicing the DMAIC approach to gain significant improvement using any of the available tools.

Statistical tools are powerful and can help in solving chronic problems, but process knowledge is paramount. Experience teaches us that most of the tools used in solving problems are simple and easy to learn. Even when statistics are needed, people often get mired in the technique instead of learning how to benefit from its application.

Each tool has its purpose and method. Learn the intent of using each tool first, then find an easy way to use it, and do not get caught up with the statistics. If the problem is complex and very critical, seek a trained statistician to join the problem-solving team instead of attempting to train everyone to become a statistician. In most cases, the statistical thinking and simple application of the statistical tools are most helpful in solving the problem.

In this chapter, key tools (as summarized in Table 4.1) in each DMAIC phase are presented in a simplified manner. These tools are very useful, simple, and virtually statistics-free.

Where statistics are important to include, we have approximated them such that the focus is on using the *concept* to make the right decision.

Process improvement can be realized by either changing the average performance or reducing the inconsistency. When changing the process average, process adjustments are utilized. When variance or inconsistency has to be reduced, a process capability study is conducted. In other words, improving process means is somewhat easier than reducing the variability in the process. The most important aspect of problem solving is to become cognizant of process average and variance, which is the square of the standard deviation.

Table 4.1: Stat-Free DMAIC Tool Application Matrix

Phase	Tools	Brief Description
D	Project Priority Index	PPI = (Benefit/Cost) X (Probability of Success/Time to complete in years) Time ≤ .5 **Estimated Savings/Cost ≥ 2.0** **Recommended PPI ≥ 4.0**
D	Pareto	A graphical tool to prioritize various defects to identify the most important one
D	Process Map	A graphical description of activities and decision points
D	Kano's Analysis	A graphical tool to identify customer critical requirements, including customers' 'love to have' requirements

D	SIPOC	An excellent tabular capture of most of the process constraints
D	CTQ	Operational critical-to-quality characteristics related to the customer expectation
D	Project Charter	Project plan with clearly-defined goals and milestones
M	Cost of Quality	Breakdown of product or service cost related to appraisal, failures and prevention
M	DPU	A product measurement, which is a ratio of the number of defects observed per unit verified
M	Yield	The percent of process output with no error or defect.
M	DPMO	A process measurement, which is the DPU normalized to the product or process complexity
M	Sigma Level	A business measurement, estimated from DPMO, commonly used for benchmarking
M	Average	Typical performance
M	Range	Range of performance (maximum – minimum)
M	Standard Deviation	More accurate range of performance; 'stat free' estimate = range/6
M	Statistical Thinking	Ability to distinguish assignable causes from random causes of variation
A	Root Cause Analysis	Fishbone diagram consisting of 4M's – Material (information), Machine (tools), Method

		(practice), and Mind power/Skills
A	FMEA	Failure Mode and Effects Analysis for anticipating problems
A	Scatter Plot	Graphical display of relationship between output (dependent) and input (independent) variables
A	Visual Regression Analysis	Estimate of relationship between input and output variables
I	Component Search	To identify the defective part in an assembly by exchanging the questionable part between 'good' and 'bad' units
I	Comparative Tests - Improving Means	Evaluating significance of shift or change in the process means
I	Comparative Tests - Improving Variance	Ratio of variances between the current and reduced variances
I	Full Factorial Experiment	Evaluating various combinations of multiple variables to determine the right combination for best performance. Total combinations = level to the power variables (L^V, e.g., $2^3 = 8$)
C	Process Thinking (4P Model)	A logical building block of the process management for achieving excellence. 4P => Prepare 4Ms,

		Perform Well, Perfect on target, Progress by reducing inconsistencies
C	Management Review	A review meeting led by the leader to ensure targeted performance is achieved and to identify necessary actions to sustain improved performance
C	Control Chart	Graphical tool to sustain normal (without known problems) behavior of the process
C	Scorecard	Measure of business performance for identifying new opportunities

A. Define - Tools

1. Project Priority Index (PPI) – Working on the right
project is critical to deploy limited resources. PPI helps in
prioritizing multiple projects based upon the estimated
savings (S) by solving the problem, initial and recurring cost
of solving the problem (C), time (T) to complete the project
to determine the solution which is ready for implementation,
and probability (P) of solving the problem successfully. PPI
is calculated as below:

$$PPI \quad = \quad (Savings/Cost) \times (P/T)$$

Table 4.2 shows an example of the projects competing for
prioritization:

Table 4.2: Competing Projects for Prioritization

Project	Potential Saving ($)	Cost to Complete ($)	Prob. of Success	Time to Complete (Year)	PPI
Defect Reduction	4,000,000	500,000	0.8	0.5	12.8
Inventory Reduction	1,000,000	100,000	0.75	1.0	7.5
Machine Utilization	200,000	150,000	0.4	0.75	.71

Given that multiple opportunities exist, the above analysis
shows that the Machine Utilization project can wait, while
the defect reduction and inventory reduction opportunities
can be realized.   Six Sigma projects are expected to
contribute to the bottom line in the short term by scoping
projects such that risks are minimized and time to complete
is reduced to about six months. Of course, the benefit-to-

cost ratio must be worth the commitment of limited precious resources. Based on the available resources, the management decides to initiate the defect reduction project or the inventory reduction project or both. The major Six Sigma projects must be approved by an authorized management representative(s) to ensure success.

2. Pareto Principle – Vifredo Pareto was an Italian economist who observed that 80 percent of income in Italy was received by 20 percent of the population. This principle was generalized by Joseph Juran, the quality guru, and it applies to most real-life situations such as:

➢ 20% of the customers provide 80% of the revenue
➢ 80% of the customer complaints arise from 20% of the products
➢ 80% of deaths occur due to 20% of known diseases

The 80:20 correlation is a symbolic representation of the Pareto principle. In reality it may be 75:25 or 85:15, but the basic intent remains the same. The Pareto principle implies the 'vital few and trivial many' concept, or that all things are not equally important.

The Pareto principle is a graphical display of categorical data in descending order based on the frequency of occurrence. A Pareto chart shows the tallest bar on the left, thus implying the most significant opportunity

The Pareto principle is a wonderful tool to utilize in making decisions between importance and convenience. Human nature is to work on convenient things instead of working on important things. Using the Pareto principle, we can always seek the most important opportunity to tackle and generate a great return on investment.

The following represents customer complaints in a call center operation:

Customer Complaints	Frequency/ year
Customer hold time	178
Wrong product supplied	16
Wrong invoice	39
Delay in credit processing	112
Bad product	12
Delay in warranty product	98
Rude customer service agent	8
Call drop	27

Figure 4.1 shows the Pareto chart with a cumulative line for the above data. One can see that the following three issues are the major (79.2%) sources of customer complaints:

1.   Excessive customer hold time
2.   Credit not processed in time
3.   Warranty product not returned in time

The normal tendency is to take care of the rude customer service agent(s) or form a task force to attack bad product issues.   The Pareto analysis, however, directs the limited resources to attack customer hold time first and the delay in credit processing issues with higher priority.

At the personal level, when we have a million things to do and are unable to decide what to work on, we can apply the Pareto principle, decide to work on the most important activity, and accomplish a lot.

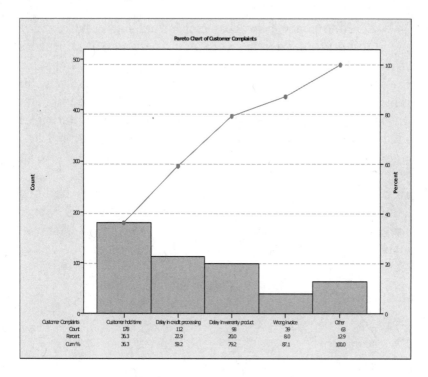

Figure 4.1 Pareto Analysis of Customer Complaints
(Ref: Minitab software)

3. Process Mapping – A process is a set of activities that
transforms inputs into the outputs.   Any business is a
collection of processes, and process mapping helps to
identify various processes and controls for consistency and
performance.   A process requires material/information, a
method/approach, machines/tools and people/skills for
achieving the target performance.   Without an established
process map or corresponding procedure, it is difficult to
ensure repeatability of a process, and dependability of its
outcome, as the process becomes more dependent on people,
thus leaving it prone to inconsistency.

In the Define phase, a process map establishes a baseline or the starting point for improvement. Analysis of the process map identifies disconnects or inefficient process steps for improvement. A process map also helps its users in developing a common understanding of the process and ensures reproducibility. Sometimes visual representation of the process provides the impetus for a number of improvement ideas.

In constructing a process map, a standard set of symbols is used for consistency and ease of interpretation. Symbols may vary from company to company. Figure 4.2 shows standard symbols used in preparing the process map.

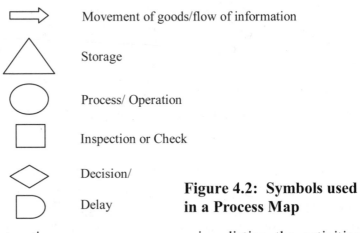

Movement of goods/flow of information

Storage

Process/ Operation

Inspection or Check

Decision/

Delay

Figure 4.2: Symbols used in a Process Map

Constructing a process map requires listing the activities, sequencing the activities, identifying checkpoints, and then drawing the process map using company-specified standard symbols. The following example shows activities and a process map for picking up food at a drive-through restaurant. The process steps are:

1.   Drive the car to the drive-through lane
2.   Wait for your turn
3.   Check the menu and decide what to order
4.   Order the items
5.   Wait for your turn
6.   Pay at the counter
7.   Pick up the food
8.   Verify contents
9.   If order is correct, leave
10. If order is incorrect, get the right one, and leave

Figure 4.3 shows the process map that depicts the drive-through process:

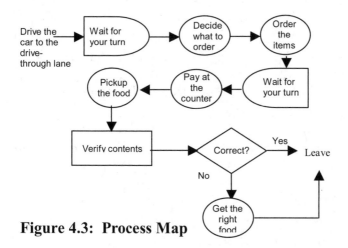

Figure 4.3: Process Map

4. Kano's Analysis - Noritaki Kano developed a model to understand the customer requirements in the following three categories:

Unspoken/Assumed Requirements: Assumed requirements are those requirements the customers assume to be present in any product or service.   For example when we stay at a hotel, we assume towels are in the bathroom, and a bed is in the room.

Spoken Customer Requirements: These are the requirements that the customer has specified. For example at the same hotel, the customer asks for an Internet connection, a business center for printing documents, or a restaurant for meals.

Unspoken Customer Desires: These are the requirements that customers realize when they interact with the product or service – what they 'love to have' for convenience and comfort that is unexpected.   For example, when customers check into a hotel room and find complementary cookies, a drink, chocolates, breakfast, or access to the Internet, they love it. These are the requirements which make their stay at the hotel memorable.

The above three requirements, as shown in Figure 4.4, are explained below:

a. Fulfilling basic requirements does not improve the customer satisfaction, but the absence of assumed requirements can lead to upset customers.

b. Meeting specific requirements satisfies the customer directly but does not earn customer loyalty.   Such products or services are price-sensitive.

c.   Delivering 'love to have' features or services
        excites customers to the point that they are
        willing to pay a premium, and spread the word
        around to potential customers, and earns loyalty
        for repeat or increased business.

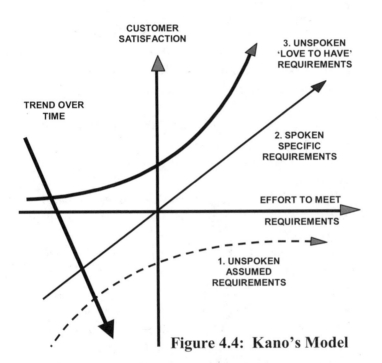

Figure 4.4: Kano's Model

Over time, the 'love to have' requirements become the
assumed requirements. Industry leaders tend to introduce
'love to have' features and services over the average
companies. To deliver 'love to have' features and services,
suppliers must care to listen to customers' total experience
and be creative in delivering these 'love to have' features

and services cost effectively. At one point, for example, the cup holder or air bags in the car used to be exciting features, but today they have become standard features and thus are assumed.

5. SIPOC – SIPOC stands for **S**upplier, **I**nput, **P**rocess, **O**utput and **C**ustomer. SIPOC enables the ability to identify various constraints and players that may contribute to the success of the process as well as problems associated with the process. While completing the SIPOC, the following issues shown in various columns are addressed:

> ➤ What key process steps are required to produce the desired output (Process)?
> ➤ What are the major outcomes of the process (Output)?
> ➤ Who receives the outputs of this process (Customer)?
> ➤ What inputs are required to perform the process activities (Input)?
> ➤ What or who is the source of inputs to the process (Supplier)?

Table 4.3 shows SIPOC for two internal safety-related processes. One of the critical aspects of completing a SIPOC is the input column, which should address the 4Ms: material or information, machine or tools, method or procedures, and manpower or people skills.

Table 4.3: SIPOC Examples for Safety Processes

Supplier (5)	Input (4)	Process (1)	Output (2)	Customer (3)
Safety department PPE suppliers Safety department Production	Safety training Personal protective equipment (PPE) Safety Procedure/ work instructions Trainers	Employee comes to work	Employee Safety Good housekeeping	Employee
Publications Safety department Specified location	Laws Emergency contacts Reporting documents First Aid kits First Aid Guidelines	Handling of unsafe incidents	Safety violation report Remedial Action	Manage-ment Safety committee OSHA Employee

The above SIPOC lists all the issues involved with the Safety process steps, ensuring complete knowledge of the process and an improved ability to investigate the process for remedying various problems associated with it.

6. Critical to Quality (CTQ) - Identifying the customer is a critical step before we can determine the customer's critical requirements. The objective is to understand customers':

> ➢ Desires
> ➢ Demands

> ➢ Needs

Once the customer requirements are known (specifically the spoken and 'love to have' requirements), one can transform them into critical-to-quality or CTQ requirements (called CTQs).

The development of a CTQ starts with a general customer requirement into the supplier's product or performance requirements, which in turn is converted into the operational performance characteristics (called CTQs). Figure 4.5 shows the development of a CTQ.

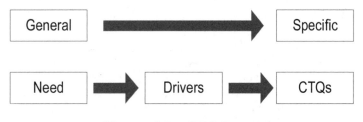

Figure 4.5: CTQ Development

For example, when ordering a meal at a restaurant, customer's drivers for ordering the meal include delivery time (e.g., 10-15 minutes), price (e.g., reasonable and affordable), and taste (e.g., must be good to eat). Figure 4.6 shows this example pictorially.

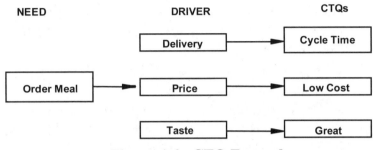

Figure 4.6: CTQ Example

The restaurant considers the customer's needs, prepares its recipe, selects ingredients, and establishes processes that meet the customer's expectation. The customer's process measures or CTQs may include cycle time, specified cost, and great taste.

7. Project Charter - A project charter is a written roadmap that:

 ➤ Documents the business case, including cost and benefit analysis as well as the financial impact
 ➤ Defines the problem to be addressed by the project
 ➤ Clarifies the project scope
 ➤ States the goal
 ➤ Defines the roles of the team members
 ➤ Establishes the timeline, milestones and key deliverables
 ➤ Identifies resources and other requirements

The Project Charter is an effective project planning tool that is referenced throughout the project and is updated as the project progresses. It is a single, consolidated plan that lays the foundation for how the project will be structured as well as how it will be managed in terms of change control, oversight, and issue resolution. The Project Charter helps in the following ways:

> ➤ The team goals are aligned with the organizational goals
> ➤ The team obtains full management commitment
> ➤ The team is aware of the project goals and boundaries
> ➤ The team can remain focused on the defined goals

B. Measure - Tools

1. Cost of Quality – The cost of quality (COQ) is the total cost incurred in the pursuit of quality or in performing quality-related activities.   Figure 4.7 shows the three components of COQ:

      a. Prevention Costs
      b. Appraisal Costs, and
      c. Failure Costs

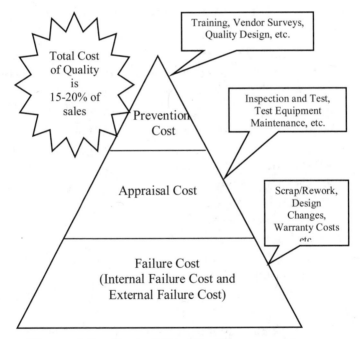

Figure 4.7: Cost of Quality Components

Prevention cost is associated with the planning, designing, implementing and monitoring of a quality system that prevents the occurrence of other failures. Following are the examples of prevention cost:

> Planning
> Capability Studies
> Design Reviews
> Field Testing
> Vendor Surveys and Evaluation
> Procedure Writing
> Training
> Market Analysis

Appraisal cost is associated with measuring, reviewing, inspecting, verifying, evaluating and checking products, services, process outputs, or materials to assure conformance to quality requirements. It is a cost of conformance. Following are the examples of appraisal cost:

> Product Audits
> Drawing Review
> Final Inspection
> In-Process Inspection
> Laboratory Testing
> Personnel Testing
> Receiving Inspection
> Shipping Inspection

Failure cost is broken into two elements: internal failure cost and external failure cost. Internal failure cost is any cost incurred in handling the product, service, software, or solution that does not meet requirements. Internal failure costs are not paid by the customer. Internal failure cost is a cost of non-performance. The examples of internal failure cost include:

> Failure Analysis
> Post Mortem
> Redesign
> Re-inspection
> Repair Costs
> Retesting
> Rework
> Scrap Allowances
> Engineering Changes
> Requirements Changes

External failure cost is any cost incurred in handling field failures. This cost is also not paid by the customer and is a cost of non-conformance. The examples of external failure cost include:

> Customer Dissatisfaction
> Equipment Downtime
> Excess Inventory
> Excess Travel Expense
> Excess Material Handling
> Penalties
> Pricing Errors

In any organization, various quality costs can be estimated as a percent of COQ as follows:

Prevention Cost	01 – 15%
Appraisal Cost	15 – 60%

Internal Failure Cost   10 – 35%
External Failure Cost   05 – 15%

The intent of analyzing cost of quality is to deploy sufficient resources in prevention as well as minimize the overall cost of quality. Prevention, Appraisal and Failure costs are also grouped together and labeled as Cost of Poor Quality (COPQ).

For example, the following quality-related costs were identified in a software company:

a. Inspection Wages $ 10,000
b. Quality Planning $ 30,000
c. User Requirement Verification $ 25,000
d. Software repair and rework $ 78,000
e. Final product test $ 95,000
f. Retest and troubleshooting $ 49,000
g. Customer support cost $ 195,000

Failure cost   = $ 49,000 + $ 195,000 = $ 244,000
Appraisal cost   = $ 10,000 + $ 25,000 + $ 78,000 +
                         $ 95,000
                    = $ 208,000
Prevention cost   = $ 30,000

The cost of poor quality should be examined as a percentage of profit instead of as a percentage of sales. The cost of poor quality comes directly from the corporate profit.

2. DPU – **D**efect **P**er **U**nit is an important and easy-to-implement product or service performance measure that corresponds to the field failures. The higher the DPU, the more field failures will be experienced by the customer.

Unit: A process output that can be a product, material, assembly, report, solution, service, or information.

Defect: A deviation of customer-specified characteristics of a product from its intended target beyond allowed tolerances leading to customer dissatisfaction.

Thus, DPU is defined as:

$$\frac{\text{Total number of defects observed in the inspected/verified units}}{\text{Total number of units inspected/verified}}$$

We are using about *defects* and not the *defective units* (i.e., one defective unit may have multiple defects). While yield talks about the number of defect-free units to the total number of units, DPU takes into account the number of defects.

For example, the following data were collected at a process for a week:

Day	Units produced	Total defective units	Total defects observed
1	100	5	8
2	100	4	9
3	100	7	14
4	100	6	10
5	100	4	12
Total	**500**	**26**	**53**

The data indicate that the yield for the process is: (500 – 26)/500 (i.e., 94.8%) while the DPU is: 53/500 (i.e., 0.106).

In the case of multiple processes in an operation, the overall yield of a process, called Rolled Throughput Yield (RTY), is equal to the multiplication of individual process yields. The following diagram shows a three-step process with its yields:

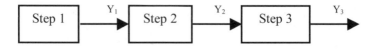

For this process the Rolled Throughput Yield (RTY) is:

RTY = Y1 x Y2 x Y3

The following equations represent the formulae for calculations:

First Pass Yield = e^{-DPU}

where 'e' represents the EXP function in MS Excel.

In the absence of easily-available defect data, one can estimate DPU using the following equation:

Estimated DPU = -LN (Yield%/100)

where LN is a natural log function available in MS Excel.

3. DPMO – DPMO is an abbreviation for **D**efect **P**er **M**illion **O**pportunities. Opportunity is the number of ways the defect or error can occur. DPMO is defined as:

$$\frac{DPU \times 1,000,000}{\text{Average number of opportunities for defect per unit}}$$

When we order pizza, for example, following are some of the ways a defect may occur:

I. Wrong crust
II. Cold pizza
III. Wrong invoice
IV. Bad taste
V. Dirty packaging
VI. Wrong toppings
VII. Late delivery
VIII. Rude behavior of delivery person

Hence eight opportunities exist for defects in delivering pizza to a customer. Table 4.4 represents the data collected at a pizza store:

Table 4.4: Frequency of Defects

Source of defect	Total pizzas delivered	Frequency
Wrong product delivered	1,000	8
Cold pizza	1,000	25
Wrong invoice	1,000	15
Bad taste	1,000	5
Bad packaging	1,000	45
Wrong toppings	1,000	12
Late delivery	1,000	78
Rudeness of delivery person	1,000	3
Total	*1000*	*191*

Therefore,

$$\text{DPU} \quad = 191/1000, \text{ or } 0.191, \text{ and}$$
$$\text{DPMO} = (0.191 \times 1{,}000{,}000)/8 \qquad = 23{,}875$$

One can see that DPMO normalizes DPU for opportunities for error, or the complexity of the process.

4. Sigma Level – Sigma level represents a measure of excellence. The higher the Sigma level, the better the quality. Sigma level is determined for the calculated DPMO as shown in Table 4.5 below.

Table 4.5: DPMO vs. Sigma Level Conversion

Sigma Level	DPMO	Sigma Level	DPMO	Sigma	DPMO
1.00	697,700	2.00	308,700	2.25	226,627
2.50	158,655	2.75	105,650	3.00	66,807
3.25	40,059	3.50	22,750	3.75	12,224
4..00	6,210	4.25	2,980	4.50	1350
4.75	577	5.00	233	5.25	88
5.50	32	5.75	11	6.00	3.4

If the estimated Sigma level is below 2.5, the process or business has serious problems which must be addressed outside the score of Six Sigma. Typical Sigma values for uninitiated and normally-working processes are expected to be about 2.5 to 3.5. The Sigma level for a well-run process may be about 3.5 to 4.5. The Sigma level corresponding to the DPMO of 23,975 is about 3.5.

Table 4.5 indicates that required improvement from three to four Sigma is 10 times, from four to five Sigma is about 30 times, and from five to six Sigma is about 70 times. Thus, the total improvement required from three Sigma to six Sigma is greater than 20,000 times.

Knowing the amount of improvement required to achieve Six Sigma level performance, only processes that are life-threatening to individuals or businesses must achieve Six Sigma level performance. However, achieving Six Sigma level performance for any process must make economic sense.

5. Average/Median – The typical or most likely value of an outcome is called the average. The average is calculated by the sum of data divided by the data count. The average value sometimes can be misleading if data are centered toward the tail ends.

For skewed data or subjective data, it is better to use the Median, which is a value that divides the data count in half. In other words, 50% of the data points are below and 50% of the data points are above the median. The median is determined by sorting the data and identifying the middle value for an odd number of data points, or the average of two middle values for an even number of data points.

6. Range – The average value is insufficient information about the process data. The average may appear to be right on target; but data may be all over the map. Range is a simple measure of dispersion in the data. In business processes, such dispersion represents inconsistency or variation in the process. The range is determined by calculating the difference between **maximum and minimum values.**

7. Variance/Standard Deviation – While calculating range, we use two data points irrespective of the size of the data set. If one has three or three million data points, range only uses two data points: the maximum and minimum values. Range is generally a more sensitive measure for smaller data sets.

Variance is another measure of dispersion in the process. It is calculated using all data points and thus is a better measure of process variation. The variance is calculated by summing the square of the difference between data points and the average value and dividing it by the data count. For example, for four values, variance can be calculated as follows:

$$\text{Variance} = \text{Sum } \{(X_1\text{-average})^2 + (X_2\text{-average})^2 + (X_3\text{-average})^2 + (X_4\text{-average})^2\}/ 4$$

Standard deviation is the square root of variance. Standard deviation is used in predicting chances of an event based on predefined statistical distributions, such as Normal distribution or Poisson distribution.

MS Excel-like software programs have built-in functions to calculate standard deviation. Standard deviation can be estimated by dividing the range by six (range/6). This approximation of standard deviation can be used while making some decisions about a typical business process. For critical situations, calculating the actual standard deviation is desirable to minimize the risk due to guess work.

$$\text{Standard Deviation} = \text{Sqrt (Variance)}$$
$$\text{Estimated Standard Deviation} = \text{Range}/6$$

8. Statistical Thinking – In order to know more about the process behavior, the average and standard deviation of that process behavior must be known. In a statistical sense, several distributions allow us to determine the likelihood of a situation, such as the occurrence of good product or the occurrence of defect. One of the commonly-known distributions is the Normal distribution as shown in Figure 4.8. The Normal distribution looks like a bell-shaped curve representing occurrence of events. Thus, many data points show occurrence of events in the middle and a few points at the tail ends of the Normal distribution. As seen in Figure 4.8, extensive work has been done to predict probabilities associated with the Normal Distribution based on the knowledge of average and standard deviation.

To determine the probability, one needs to locate the data point representing an event on the bell-shaped curve. The distance between the process mean, or the center of the bell-shaped curve, and the data point in terms of standard deviation is called the 'z' value. In other words, the 'z' value is the number of standard deviations away from the process mean.

To make it easy for estimating the likelihood of an event, remember the following: Likelihood within one standard deviation around the mean is about $2/3^{rd}$, within two standard deviations around the mean is 95%, and within three standard deviations around the mean is approaching 100%.

The significance of knowing the likelihood of events within one, two or three standard deviations is that variation occurring between two standard deviations with a chance of 95% is considered to be common due to random uncontrolled variables. The variation occurring with a chance of 5% outside two standard deviations is called exception due to assignable variables.

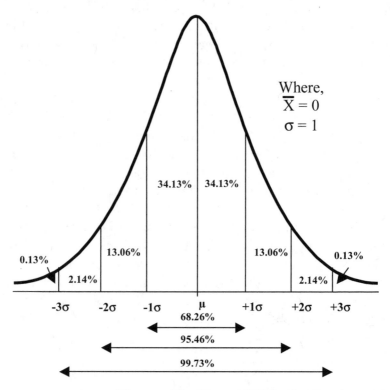

Figure 4.8: Normal Distribution

Statistical thinking means understanding the nature of inconsistencies based on frequency of occurrence. If the inconsistency in a process is excessive due to random variables, a thorough process capability study must be conducted to improve the process. If the inconsistency is incidental with an exception, the process is adjusted to improve the process.

In order to reduce common variation, in other words, process knowledge must be enhanced significantly. Such processes have a larger standard deviation. To reduce exceptional variation, certain process parameters are adjusted. Such processes have shift in the process mean of a sample(s). If exceptional variation is not remedied, it becomes part of the common variation and is thus inherent in the process.

The common variation is inherent in the process due to many variables, while the exceptional variation is introduced in the process by a specific variable or a few variables.

For example, when one drives to work in the morning, a certain time to arrive at work is expected. If someone asks, "How long does it take to get to work," the answer may be 30 minutes plus/minus 5 minutes. The give and take of 5 minutes around the typical time represents a 95% chance of happening. However, due to an accident one day you are late by 20 minutes. That late arrival is an exception, as the excessive delay occurred due to a known assignable cause.

To reduce the typical commuting time of 30 minutes, one needs to think of improving process capability either by changing the route, using a different vehicle, or working from home (e.g., virtual commuting). To reduce the exceptional delay of 20 minutes, one may plan to leave early to avoid the peak traffic hour when an accident is likely to occur.

This explanation initially appears to be counterintuitive. We think that when an event occurs rarely, it happens by chance (implying small chance). In statistical thinking, however, everything happens by chance. The degree of chance is what separates the random events from assignable events.

The causes that contribute to random variation are difficult to identify, control and change. The causes that contribute to assignable variation are easier to identify (assign), control and change. In controlling processes, the objective is to maintain the process in statistical control (i.e., without any assignable variables).

C. Analyze - Tools

1. Root Cause Analysis – Root cause analysis is an excellent tool to identify potential causes of a given problem. In 1943, Dr. Kaoru Ishikawa, president of the Musashi Institute of Technology in Tokyo first utilized the root cause analysis diagram. Therefore, the tool is sometimes called an Ishikawa diagram or a fishbone diagram because of its resemblance to the skeleton of a fish.

Root cause analysis has the following advantages:

➢ Eliminates trivial causes of a problem
➢ Establishes inter-relationships among various causes
➢ Simple to use and easy to complete
➢ Graphical format rather than statistical tool
➢ Increased process knowledge
➢ Cross-functional effort and improved communication

A clear definition of the problem forms the basis for effective root cause analysis. While performing a root cause analysis, we explore What, Where, When, Why, How, and How Many:

➢ What - description, symptoms, and severity
➢ Where - part #, location, situations, geographic
➢ When - time and frequency of the problem
➢ Why - explanation contributing to the problem
➢ How - mode of operation or activities
➢ How many or how much - magnitude of the problem

The Ishikawa diagram, as shown in Figure 4.9, consists of the four major branches, namely material, machine, method and manpower. The manpower implies skills of the person doing the work, rather than one's intention. Correspondingly for non-manufacturing operations, the 4Ms represent information, tools, methodology and competency.

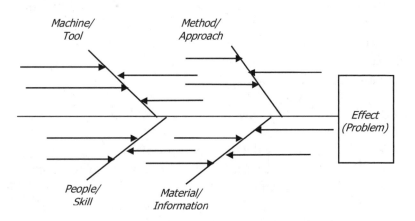

Figure 4.9: Ishikawa Diagram

Conducting the root cause analysis involves the following activities:

1. Form a cross functional team
2. Define the problem clearly
3. Label the box with the problem or the effect
4. Attach four major branches and label them
5. Brainstorm and list potential causes for major categories, building on each other's ideas (10 – 15 causes for a simple problem, 20 – 30 causes for a complex problem)
6. Prioritize and select at least one major potential cause on each branch. If necessary, select more than one on each branch. Circle the vital causes.

7. Probe critical causes by asking 'why' until an action can be defined to remedy the inconsistency
8. Assign responsibility and a completion date for each action item

Figure 4.10 shows an example of root cause analysis of the safety problems in a company:

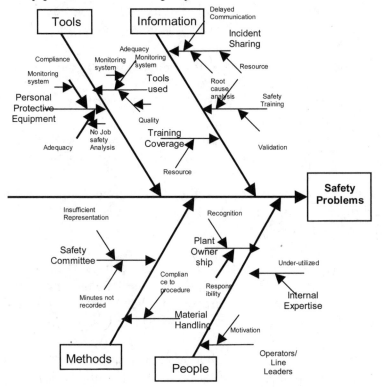

Figure 4.10: Root Cause Analysis of Safety Problems

2. FMEA – In the aerospace, automotive, railway, and pharmaceutical industries, Failure Mode and Effects

Analysis (FMEA) is a mandated activity to identify and mitigate potential risks. Similarly, for customer- or business-critical operations, FMEA can be performed to prevent anticipated problems from happening.

The FMEA process consists of the following:

> ➤ identify the potential failure modes, effects and causes associated with designing and producing a product/service
> ➤ evaluate the severity of effects, occurrence of causes, and detection of controls
> ➤ determine the risk level based on severity, occurrence and detection
> ➤ prioritize potential failures based on the risk level
> ➤ establish an action plan to mitigate significant risks

When FMEA is utilized in the design stage, it is called Design FMEA or DFMEA; at the process stage, it is called Process FMEA or PFMEA.

Severity (S) is an assessment of the seriousness of the effect of the potential failure mode to the next component, subsystem, system or customer. It applies to effects only and is rated between 1 (least severe) and 10 (most severe).

Occurrence (O) is the likelihood that a specific cause will occur. The possible failure rates are based on the anticipated failure rate(s) during the process execution. Occurrence is rated between 1 (no occurrence) and 10 (very frequent occurrence).

Detection (D) is an assessment of the ability of the process controls to detect potential causes or the subsequent failure mode before the part or system leaves the operations area. It is rated between 1 (certain detection) and 10 (no detection).

Table 4.6 provides guidelines for assessing severity, occurrence and detection.

Table 4.6: Risk Assessment Guidelines

Severity	Ranking	Occurrence of Failure	Ranking	Detection	Ranking
Hazardous without warning	10	Very High: Failure is almost inevitable (>1 in 2)	10	Absolute Uncertainty	10
Hazardous with warning	9	1 in 3	9	Very Remote	9
Very High	8	High: Repeated failures (1 in 8)	8	Remote	8
High	7	1 in 20	7	Very Low	7
Moderate	6	Moderate: Occasional failures (1 in 80)	6	Low	6
Low	5	1 in 400	5	Moderate	5
Very Low	4	1 in 2,000	4	Moderately High	4
Minor	3	Low: Relatively few failures (1 in 15,000)	3	High	3
Very Minor	2	1 in 150,000	2	Very High	2
None	1	Remote: Failure is unlikely (< 1 in 1,500,000)	1	Almost Certain	1

Ref. www.fmeainfocenter.com

Risk Priority Number (RPN) is the multiplication of S, O, and D and is used to prioritize risks.

The FMEA begins with the process map or the design block diagram. Once the process steps are listed, various potential failure modes are identified for evaluation. For each effect, potential causes are listed using the Ishikawa thinking, and the corresponding frequency of occurrence is estimated. Detection is assessed based on internal process controls or checks.

While reducing the RPN (risk priority number), one identifies actions to reduce severity, occurrence or escapes.

Table 4.7 is an example of an FMEA for safety-related activities:

Table 4.7: An Example of FMEA

Process Steps	Potential Failure Mode	Potential Effects of Failure Mode	S	Potential Causes of Failure Mode	O	Current Process Controls	D	RPN
Audit	1. Inadequate audit frequency	1. Development of unsafe conditions	6	1. Lack of institutionalized audit systems	4	1. Quarterly safety audits	7	168
	2. Low employee participation	1. No employee development	5	1. Lack of knowledge of accident prevention/ safety audit process/ tools	4	1. Team audits	5	100

Incident Reporting	1. Poor learning	1. Incident repeats 2. Low awareness	9 6	1. Absence of formal communication system to all employees	6 5	1. Safety committee 2. Safety committee	4 4	216 120
	2. Insufficient investigation	1. Root causes not eliminated	7	1. Lack of training in incident investigation	8	1. Supervisor Communica-tion	7	392

3. Scatter Plot – A scatter diagram is a graphical presentation of the relationship between two quantitative variables. It is developed by plotting the dependent variable (or the variable of interest) on the Y-Axis and the independent variable (the variable which impacts the dependent variable) on the X-Axis of a two-dimensional graph. Figure 4.11 shows the scatter diagram based on a grocery store's weekend sales (Y-Axis) and weekly advertising expense (X-Axis) data.

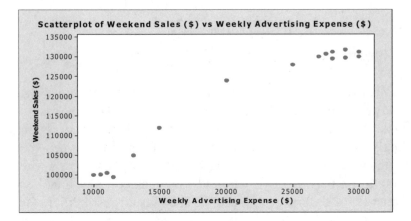

Figure 4.11: An Example of a Scatter Plot
(Refr: Minitab software)

If we were the store's manager, what conclusions can we draw looking at the graph? The upwardly-clustered observations indicate that the sales growth is positively related to advertising expense. We can also see that the graph may plateau at about $25,000 in weekly advertising expense. The relationship between the two variables can be positive or negative as shown in Figures 4.12 A, B and C.

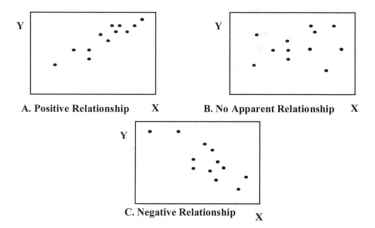

A. Positive Relationship   X   B. No Apparent Relationship   X

C. Negative Relationship   X

Figure 4.12: Relationships Depicted by Scatter Plot

4. Visual Regression Analysis – The scatter plot shows the relationship between two variables X and Y. The regression analysis quantifies the relationship.   Visual Regression Analysis allows one to evaluate the correlation between the two variables for practical purposes.   For quantifying the correlation between two variables, one can use MS Excel or statistics software programs.   The visual estimation of regression helps to gain insight into the relationship between two variables. Drawing a best-fit line between the series of points on the scatter plot allows for the determination of both a linear or non-linear relationship as well as the strength of the relationship.

If the relationship is not very strong, some important variable(s) in the analysis have been missed and must be found. The visual regression analysis helps us move quickly without complicated statistical analysis.

D. Improve - Tools

1. Component Search – Component search is a natural way of solving problems, where one swaps a part between a working and non-working unit to see if it changes the performance. The purpose of a component search experiment is to identify the likely components causing variation in the performance of a product. Typically, the component search technique can be used where the components can be exchanged without affecting the performance. Such products can be easily assembled or disassembled.

This type of experiment requires one 'good' and one 'bad' unit. The technique uses a process-of-elimination approach by switching the components, between these two units, to determine the effect of each component on the output response being measured. The objective of a component search experiment is to identify a component(s) that changes a good unit into a bad unit, and the bad unit into a good unit.

Key Assumptions

1. There are two units – one with all good parts and another with few troublesome parts.
2. The difference in the performance of the two units is significantly different and is solely caused by the difference in the component performance.
3. The process of interchanging parts does not affect the performance of units.
4. The performance can be measured and repeated any number of times without deteriorations.

To conduct a component search experiment, one must get samples of good units and defective units and then follow the steps listed below:

1. Measure the performance of the good and bad units
2. Brainstorm to identify questionable components
3. Rank troublesome parts based on the significance of their impact on the units
4. Interchange the most troublesome part between good and bad units and observe changes in performance
5. Analyze results. The following outcomes are possible:
   a. No Change - The interchanged part may not be the cause of poor performance. In this case, interchange the components back to their old state. Proceed with the next ranked part and continue with the experiment.
   b. Partial Change - The interchanged part does have marginal impact on the performance of good and bad units but is an indirect cause of the problem. Partial change represents an interaction with other components.
   c. Complete Reversal - The interchanged part was the root cause of the problem, and the performance of good and bad units is reversed.

Once a problem part or a combination of parts is identified, verification or a capping experiment must be conducted. A capping run ensures that 'all' the components which affect the difference in the product/process output are identified. The capping run is normally performed by completely interchanging all the parts that now result in the complete reversal of the product/process performance.

2. Comparative Tests – Improving Means – Normally, processes experience a problem due to some assignable causes that result in a shift in the performance of the output or product. If the problem persists and becomes chronic, then the variance is significantly affected, and the problem becomes inherent in the process. In order to improve a process, one needs to change the process mean or the process variance.

When the process mean needs to be changed, at this stage of the methodology a variable or two has/have been identified. Based on the process knowledge, the change in the variable setting is identified, and a new process is defined. However, before the process is changed in the production or operation, it must be verified. Comparative experimentation is a method to compare two process outputs for evaluating differences between their means.

This method implies that two processes exist – a current process and a better process (assuming we do not make a process worse!). For example, the current process leads to customer satisfaction of 78%, and the improved process leads to the satisfaction of 88%, 92%, 94%, 88%, 86%, 98%, 89% and 89% for eight customers.

The average customer satisfaction is 90.5% with a standard deviation of 3.93 determined using MS Excel.

In this example, we can see an improvement in customer satisfaction from 78% to 90.5%. Sometimes, seeing a change from 78% to 82% is possible. The question one must ask is this: "Is the improvement significant to sustain, or is it just sample dependent?" Thus, the change in a process is evaluated with respect to the common variation in the process and is normalized in standard deviations.

Initially, instead of a more rigorous statistical approach, calculating the ratio of change to standard deviation is recommended. If the ratio is greater than 2.0, the change can be considered significant and the process can be improved.

In other words, if a process mean is improved by greater than two standard deviations, the change can be considered significant with a reasonable and economic sample size.

Note: For finer improvement in critical processes, more rigorous statistical tests must be performed.

3. Comparative Tests – Improving Variance – When a process is chronically sick or is difficult to improve, reducing the process variance should be the focus.

Reducing process variance implies improvement in the process capability, which means a more thorough process characterization is needed to relearn the process at a new level of the performance. Once the new process recipe is identified, a verification run is conducted, and data from samples of current and better processes are collected for analysis.

To compare two variances, the F-test is used, which is a ratio of two variances as shown in the formula below:

$$F_{Calculated} \text{ Value} \quad = \quad \frac{\text{Larger Variance}}{\text{Smaller Variance}}$$

(Remember, the variance is a square of the standard deviation.)

To simplify this tool using the F-test, Table 4.8 summarizes the expected values in order to determine if reduction in variance is significant. These $F_{Expected}$ values have been simplified for practical applications and equal sample size before and after the improvement. These values are very conservative, and for precise application, consulting with a statistics professional is recommended.

Table 4.8: F-Significance Table

Sample Size	$F_{Expected}$ Value
3	20
5	10
10	5
20	3

For variance reduction to be significant,

$$F_{Calculated} \geq F_{Expected}$$

As an example, for the sample size of 10 pieces, the variance before and after improvement has been determined to be 12 and 2 respectively. Thus, $F_{Calculated} = 12/2 = 6$, which is greater than the $F_{Expected}$ value of 5. Thus, reduction in variance is statistically significant (or they are different).

Situations do occur when a sample is collected from a running process to monitor changes in the variance. A test called the Chi Squared (χ^2) Test is used to evaluate change in the process variance. In this case, the standard deviation of the process is known.

The formula to determine $\chi^2_{Calculated}$ is as follows:

$$\chi^2_{Calculated} = \frac{(n-1) \times S^2}{\sigma^2}$$

Where, (χ^2) = Chi-square variable
            n   = Sample size
            S^2 = Sample variance
            σ^2 = Known Target Variance

Table 4.9 shows the simplified significance values of the χ^2 test.

Table 4.9: χ^2-Significance Table

Sample Size	$\chi^2_{Expected}$ Value	Expected Reduction in Variability	Expected S/σ
3	.1	> 80%	< .2
5	.7	> 60%	< .4
10	3.3	> 40%	< .6
20	10	> 20%	< .8

If the is $\chi^2_{Calculated} \leq \chi^2_{Expected}$ the reduction in the process variance can be considered significant. For example, new software was developed with the target variance of 10 in defects per module. Ten modules were reviewed, and the variance in defect per module was observed to be 2.

In this case, $n = 10$
$$S^2 = 2, \text{ or } S = 1.41,$$
$$\sigma^2 = 10, \text{ or } \sigma = 3.16$$

$$\chi^2_{Calculated} = \frac{(10-1) \times 2}{10}$$
$$= 1.8$$

Since $\chi^2_{Calculated}$ 1.8 is less than $\chi^2_{Expected}$ 3.3, we can conclude that process variance has reduced significantly.

The stat free approach will include the following:

$$s/\sigma = 1.41/3/16$$
$$= .447$$

For a sample size of 10, s/σ is less than .6, as specified in Table 4.9. Thus, the process variability has been significantly reduced.

Another simple way to evaluate improvement in variance is by evaluating reduction in standard deviation. As Table 4.9 shows, the smaller the sample, the larger the reduction is expected in order to draw the conclusion about reduction in inconsistency.

4. Full Factorial Experiment – When we are unable to decide which one factor is responsible for excessive inconsistency in the process, then multiple factors may be working on the process concurrently. In such cases, our objective is to identify the effect of each variable, as well as the effect of interaction of those variables. As the number of variables increases, the challenge of finding the right combination compounds.

The complexity is manifested by the number of possible combinations to be tried out to learn about main effects and interaction among them is given by the formula L^V, where L stands for number of levels or settings of the variables, and V is the number of variables. If the number of variables is 5 and the number of levels is kept at 2, the number of trials will be 32 (2^5). This is a large number of trials at the minimum number of settings and a small number of variables.

Following are the key steps in conducting the full factorial experiment:

1. Define the experiment objective
2. Identify the key variables
3. Conduct the preliminary study of the expected response and decide the two levels
4. Conduct the experiments
   a. Determine the cells
   b. Determine the number of samples per cell
   c. Perform the experiment
   d. Record the outcomes
5. Analyze the data
6. Draw conclusions
7. Implement actions

An example follows of reducing the error rate in software development. The factors affecting the error rate are the developer's experience and the frequency of review with the user. The Six Sigma team decides to conduct experiments at the two levels of these factors as outlined below:

Developer's experience: *< 2 years*   *≥ 2 years*
User review: *Quarterly*   *Monthly*

Following are the average error rates for various combinations of factors:

User Review		< 2 years	≥ 2 years
	1/ month	47	41
	1/ quarter	51	49

< 2 years   ≥ 2 years
Developer's Experience

As evidenced in the above table, the main effect of the two factors at the error rate is outlined below:

$$
\begin{aligned}
\text{User Review} \quad &= \quad (47+41)/2 - (51+49)/2 \\
&= \quad 44 - 50 \\
&= \quad -6
\end{aligned}
$$

$$
\begin{aligned}
\text{Developer's Experience} &= \quad (49+41)/2 - (51+47)/2 \\
&= \quad 45 - 44 \\
&= \quad 1
\end{aligned}
$$

We note from the above data that the increase in the frequency of user review reduces the error rate, but higher developer's experience actually increases the error rate. These main effects can be graphically represented in Figures 4.13a and 4.13b:

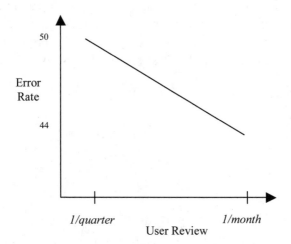

Figure 4.13a: Main Effect of User Review

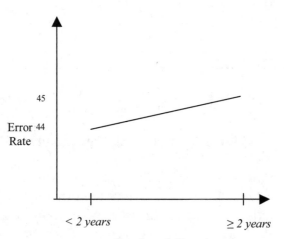

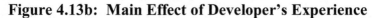

Figure 4.13b: Main Effect of Developer's Experience

By exploring the interaction, the power of the Full Factorial Experiment tool can be seen. Interaction occurs when the performance of User Review is adversely affected by an increase in the Developer's Experience. The interaction between the two variables is shown in Figure 4.14.

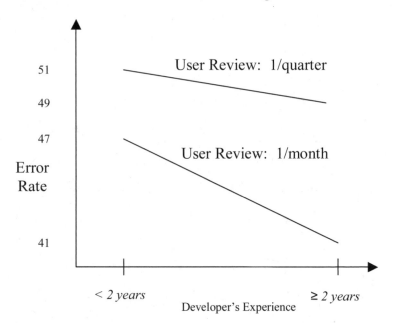

Figure 4.14: Interaction Effect

The effect of experience on the error rate depends upon the frequency of the user review. More review frequency results in a reduction in the error rate with more experience. However, less frequent review results in a decrease in the error rate, with the experience at a less rate than when more frequent review takes place. In other words, a sharper decline exists in the error rate for more experienced developers than less experienced developers. Following is a calculation of the effect of this interaction:

$$
\text{Interaction} \quad = \quad \frac{(51 + 41) - (47 + 49)}{2} \quad 2
$$

$$
= \quad 46 - 48
$$
$$
= \quad -2
$$

The following summarizes the Full Factorial experiment:

Factor	Error Rate
User Review	-6
Developer's Experience	1
Review and Experience Interaction	-2

The above analysis shows that the User Review has the most significant impact on the error rate.   Experience and interaction may not have the significant impact. In any case, a comparative experiment must be conducted just with the User Review to validate the experiment prior to implementing the process change about User Review.

For more than two variables, more complicated factorial experiments can be analyzed using commercially-available statistical software programs.

E. Control - Tools

1. Process Thinking (4-P Model of Process Excellence) –
The 4-P model of process excellence is comprised of four
phases:

1.   Prepare
2.   Perform
3.   Perfect
4.   Progress

The 4P model has incorporated the wisdom of quality
management gurus such as Ishikawa, Juran, Taguchi,
Deming, and Shewhart.   Ishikawa focused on preparation,
Juran focused on performance or execution, Taguchi focused
on target or perfection, Deming focused on reducing
variability or progress, and Shewhart focused on the entire
cycle of process control.

The 4-P Process Model focuses on the quality of inputs,
converted by a set of value-added activities, to produce an
output that is *on target* for the customer.   If the target is
missed, inconsistency is reduced by modifying the inputs or
activities.

The Prepare step represents assurance of good inputs to the
process.   The inputs consist of Ishikawa's 4Ms – material,
machine, method and manpower.   The goal is to ensure that
these 4Ms are received correctly by the process.

The Perform step implies that the process is well-defined,
mistake-proofed and understood for consistent and effective

execution. The Perfect step ensures that the process output is on target.

If the process output is not on target, the gap from the target must be recognized. The Progress step leads to improvement in the process and its outputs by reducing variation around the target.

By continually applying the 4-P cycle, companies can reengineer a process to achieve desired results by the customer through a better process instead of a better inspection of the product. The 4-P model is shown in Figure 4.15.

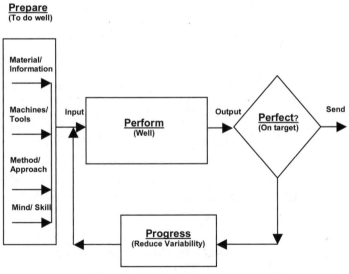

Figure 4.15: The 4-P Model

For example, the process of getting a driver's license is shown in Figure 4.16.

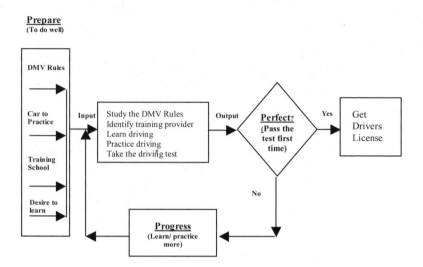

Figure 4.16: The 4-P Model for obtaining a Driver's License

2. Management Review – The purpose of management review is to evaluate the effectiveness of the Six Sigma initiative by reviewing the progress and results towards intended objectives, missed goals, and the status of corrective actions. Table 4.10 can be used to record observations in the management review meeting. Conduct the management review of the Six Sigma initiative regularly as a commitment to the Six Sigma initiative.

Table 4.10: Template for Management Review

Projects	Results	Gap	Cause	Remedy

An engaging and challenging management review is the soul of implementing the Six Sigma initiative successfully.

3. Control Chart – The control chart is a method to monitor the statistical nature of a process and identify when the process has been affected with an assignable cause. Ultimately a control chart is a device to maintain the normal distribution of the process output. When the distribution is disturbed, the process must be adjusted to remove the assignable cause and bring the process back in statistical control.

All assignable causes must be removed before using a control chart to monitor a process. Otherwise the control chart will highlight out-of-control situations too many times and thus most likely be ignored.

Control charts are classified into two categories based on the type of data used for controlling the process. Attribute control charts are used when attribute data are collected, and variable control charts are used when variable data are collected. Various types of control charts are as follows:

Attribute Control Charts

u chart: average number of DPU in a subgroup
np chart: number of defective units in a sample
p chart: the percent or proportion defective in a subgroup
c chart: the number of defects in a subgroup

Variable Control Charts

X bar-R chart: mean and range of subgroup size ≤ 5

X bar-s chart: mean and std. dev. for subgroup size ≥ 5
X-R (or MR - Moving Range*) chart:* when plotting
individual points

Figure 4.17 shows an example of a control chart.

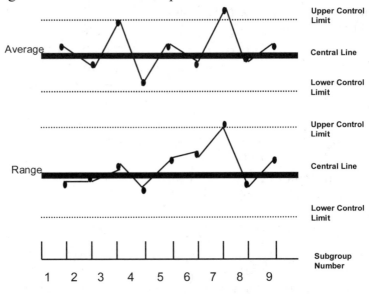

Figure 4.17: An Example of a Control Chart

Irrespective of the type of control chart, the basic rules of maintaining statistical controls are the same. The rules are established based on the probabilities of having points in areas between the number of standard deviations and the mean. The main difference is the method employed to calculate control limits using different formulae.

Interpreting control charts correctly is necessary to adjust the process appropriately. Rules are designed to detect patterns, trends, shifts, drift, and non-normal behavior. Following are commonly-used rules for determining out of control conditions:

1. Data point is beyond control limits.
2. Nine points in a row on a side of the center line.
3. Six points in a row increasing or decreasing.
4. Fourteen points in a row alternating up and down.
5. Two out of three points in a row beyond two Sigma.
6. Four out of five points in a row beyond one Sigma.
7. Fifteen points in a row within one Sigma.
8. Eight points in a row on both sides of the center line within two Sigma.

We can note from our example that the process is not under control, because data points (corresponding to subgroup seven) in both the average and range charts are outside the upper control limit.

4. Scorecard – One of the challenges is to continually identify opportunities for improvement that can have impact on the top and bottom line. The Six Sigma Business Scorecard (Gupta, 2006) was developed to assess a business in its entirety for its performance in achieving sustained profitable growth. The scorecard can be considered an extension of the Balanced Scorecard, but it is also fundamentally different in many ways. The purpose of the Six Sigma Business Scorecard is to continually identify opportunities for dramatic improvement, and it leads to the overall Sigma level for an organization. The basic tenet of the Six Sigma Business Scorecard is to have the leadership inspire employees, managers drive improvement, and employees strive to innovate.

The Six Sigma Business Scorecard aggregates all corporate performance measurements into seven elements as listed below:

1. Leadership and profitability (LAP)
2. Management and improvement (MAI)
3. Employees and innovation (EAI)
4. Purchasing and supplier management (PSM)
5. Operational execution (OPE)
6. Sales and distribution (SAD)
7. Service and growth (SAG)

These ten elements correspond to ten measurements that are added up to establish a Business Performance Index (BPIn). Ten measurements and their significance to the BPIn are listed below:

Measurement	Abbreviation	Significance
1. Employees recognized for excellence	LAP	15
2. Profitability	LAP	15
3. Rate of Improvement – all departments	MAI	20
4. Recommendation per employee	EAI	10
5. Total Spend/Sales	PSM	5
6. Suppliers' Defect Rate (Sigma)	PSM	5
7. Operational Cycle Time Variance	OPE	5
8. Process Defect Rate (Sigma)	OPE	5
9. New Business ($)/Total Sales ($)	SAD	10
10. Customer Satisfaction	SAG	10
	Total:	100

For each measurement, a score is assigned in a percentage, multiplied by its significance, and assessed for its contribution to BPIn. The BPIn represents the goodness of the business and identifies the gap from the ideal performance, thus identifying opportunities for improvement.

BPIn for a Dow 30 Company based on the 2003 data was estimated to be about 70%, implying several opportunities exist to improve BPIn greater than 70%.

STAT FREE SIX SIGMA MEASUREMENTS

Six Sigma requires an understanding of the measurement system in order to be applied effectively. We need to ensure that a practical measurement system is in place to help improve the process much faster rather than debating the accuracy of the measurement system. In Six Sigma methodology, the absolute value of measurements is less critical than the rate of improvement. All organizations consist of processes; all processes are a collection of activities. The main objective of the program is to improve a process faster than the variance due to a questionable measurement method.

The first challenge of the process is to identify what aspects of the business should be measured. What is the simplest way to determine important aspects? If the quality of a product or service is important, ask *why* quality is important to the company. The following questions may help to explore and identify desired measurements:

> ➢ Business objectives: Why is a product, process or business characteristic important to business?
> ➢ Success factors: What goals should be achieved?
> ➢ Input Measurements: What is needed to achieve these goals?
> ➢ Process Measurements: How are these goals achieved?

> Output Measurements: How is achievement of those goals determined?

By asking such questions, a company can identify effective measurements to ensure excellence. For service operations, answering these questions identifies the measurements and helps a company understand units, and defects per million opportunities (DPMO) to identify areas for improvement.

Application of Six Sigma Measurements

Let us look at an example of the electronic assembly that includes process steps such as picking parts from the stockroom, scheduling for automated assembly such as pick and place, soldering, testing, inspection, hand soldering, mechanical assembly, system assembly, system test and final QA. The process flow is shown in Figure 5.1.

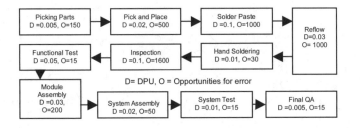

Figure 5.1 Electronics Assembly Line

The process steps, along with their DPU (D) and average number of opportunities for error (O) for each process, are identified in the flow chart. Table 5.1: Operation Quality Data shows implementation of various Six Sigma measurements.   A similar approach can be adapted for service or software operations, where each key operation is identified, and its DPU, yield, opportunities, DPMO, and Sigma level are determined.   In order to determine the overall Sigma level, all DPMOs across operations are added to obtain an overall DPMO.

Table 5.1: Operation Quality Data

Operation	DPU	Identification of opportunities	# of Opp.	DPMO	Sigma Level
Picking parts	0.005	# of unique parts picked	150	33	5.5
Pick and place	0.02	# of unique parts placed	500	40	5.4
Solder paste	0.1	# of unique pads	1000	100	5.2
Reflow	0.03	# of unique connections	1000	30	5.5
Hand Soldering	0.1	# of unique leads	30	3333	4.2
Inspection	0.1	# of unique connections and parts	1600	63	5.3
Functional test	0.05	# of steps	15	3333	4.2
Module Assembly	0.03	# of unique parts used	200	150	5.1
System Assembly	0.02	# of different modules	50	400	4.9
System Test	0.01	# of steps	15	667	4.7
Final QA	0.005	# of steps	15	333	4.9
Total				**8482**	**3.9**

For the software development process, the Sigma level can be determined by establishing performance measures at each of the following steps:
  ➢ Requirements analysis
  ➢ Software design
  ➢ Coding

➤ Testing
➤ Integration
➤ QC

Similarly we can calculate the Sigma level for an operation at a hospital by adding the DPMO for each of the following processes:

➤ Admission
➤ Pre-surgical preparation
➤ Surgery preparation
➤ Surgery
➤ Post-surgery care
➤ Follow-up
➤ Payment processing

Data Sources

Most organizations suffer from two types of problems – too much data or data that are not useful. If the right set of data is available, we can start using it to calculate the DPU for each process step. If no data are available, we can always estimate the process performance in a percentage based upon experience and feedback from customers. The process yield can be converted into DPU using the following formula:

$$DPU = -LN(\%Yield/100)$$

LN is a natural log and can be calculated using the Excel spreadsheet function {=LN (Number)}.

Corporate Sigma Level

The business is a collection of processes. When the DPMO is summed for all the processes, the business DPMO and the business Sigma level can be calculated.

Another way to determine Corporate Sigma level is using the Business Performance Index (BPIn). The Sigma level using the BPIn will have a better correlation to the top and bottom line, as the Six Sigma Business Scorecard includes all aspects of the business. The corporate DPU is calculated using the following formula:

$$DPU \quad = \quad -LN\ (BPIn\%/100)$$

The number of executives reporting to the CEO and COO are considered opportunities for error, as all decisions are made by the executives reporting to the CEO and COO. If problems or opportunities arise, the responsibility lies with these executives. Thus corporate DPMO can be calculated using the following formula:

$$DPMO \quad = \quad \frac{DPU \times 1,000,000}{\text{Number of Executives reporting to CEO and COO}}$$

We know the corporate Sigma level by looking at the DPMO to Sigma conversion in Table 4.5 (in Chapter 4). As an example, an organization has 15 executives reporting to the CEO and COO, and its current BPIn is 68%. The DPU for this organization is calculated using the MS Excel function {=-LN (BPIn/100)}.

Therefore, DPU = - LN (68/100)
= 0.385662
DPMO = (0.385662 x 1,000,000)/ 15
= 25,711
Sigma = 3.45

A DPMO of 25,711 corresponds to the Sigma level of 3.45. The leadership can now set its goals to improve the Sigma level on an annual basis rather than just continue to implement Six Sigma.

Assume for the moment that an individual is hired to implement Six Sigma who reports to the COO. The BPIn improves to 81% after one year. Then,

$DPU_{(+1 \; yr)}$ = -LN (0.81)
= 0.210721
$DPMO_{(+1 \; yr)}$ = (0.210721 x 1,000,000)/16
= 13,170
Sigma = 3.72

The DPMO has reduced by about 50%, and the corresponding Sigma level has changed from 3.45 to 3.72. Thus DPMO must continue to decrease in order to improve the Sigma level to the established annual targets.

CHAPTER SIX

SIX SIGMA AND INNOVATION

Six Sigma means quick improvement in a short period of time. Incremental and continual improvement need to be replaced with breakthrough improvement or continual reengineering. Breakthrough improvement is achieved through innovation, which is an implicit intent of Six Sigma but is often inadvertently ignored in the methodology.

Breakthrough improvement will save a lot of time and money for a company. Breaking rules through innovation is a way for breakthrough improvement. Today, due to the lack of an established process, innovation is not an element of Six Sigma training programs or methodology. This lack of training in innovation has become a challenge, because projects are postponed while "waiting for the light bulb to turn on." The companies that are strong proponents of Six Sigma move to the next project after a mere ten percent improvement in the existing project. We call this project-hopping and a missed opportunity for innovation.

The intent, strategy and methodology of Six Sigma are often not understood. An understanding of innovation should be incorporated in the body of knowledge of Six Sigma in order to achieve quick improvement in a very short time.

Innovation appears to be very much aligned with the intent and expectation of any corporate Six Sigma. When emphasizing innovation to achieve Six Sigma results, one must consider creating a culture for innovation. Innovative thinking must become an integral part of the Six Sigma initiative and must, therefore, be integrated through implementation and recognition.

Every employee in a corporation is capable of being innovative. Bringing out the ability to achieve significant improvement is an expectation that leadership must establish and seek. The intellectual participation of employees must be a leadership mantra. All good leaders see potential in their employees and exploit it as the only way to achieve sustained improvement.

Innovation begins with the intellectual involvement of employees through their ideas. The process of getting employee ideas or recommendations has been in existence for a long time. However, its effective implementation and success have been far from satisfactory.

Just like purchasing, sales, production or quality processes, innovation should become a standard in any corporation. Leadership commitment to successfully implement the innovation process must be present. An innovation must then be defined, expectations must be established, resources should be allocated, and measurements must be established to monitor innovation value. Most importantly, innovation must be incorporated into the business planning and budgeting in order to be visible on the management radar.

The first process in creating innovative thinking is to establish a good idea management program. Idea management is all about contributing toward employees' success through their company's success and by achieving improvement. Everyone will benefit by growing professionally and increasing ones earning potential.

The lack of innovative thinking at the leadership or project level is one factor that prevents significant improvement in the bottom line or process performance. Effective leaders must possess the following four skills to produce a lot of improvement quickly:

1. **Time management:** A lack of time management skills stalls the execution of any planned activity. Projects fall behind schedule because people like to work on convenient things instead of important things. People think they are busy but are unable to see any progress.

2. **Process thinking:** Process thinking relates to the 4-P model of process excellence. The Prepare stage is where we identify the inputs necessary to perform the process well. The Perform stage is where we take steps to perform tasks involved in a process. The Perfect stage is where we compare the process output with the target value. Finally, the Progress stage involves learning from the root cause analysis of deviation from the target.

3. **Statistical thinking:** Statistical thinking requires an understanding of random and assignable variation. The random variation is uncontrollable, while the assignable variation occurs because of a specific action.

Statistical thinking allows leaders to make a decision based on the understanding of the nature of variation.

4. **Innovative thinking:** Innovative thinking implies doing things differently. In order to practice innovative thinking, one must possess the process knowledge, be able to experiment with various possibilities, and see beyond the obvious by stretching the solution to achieve breakthrough improvement. If an organization plans to benefit from a Six Sigma initiative over the long term, its leaders must institutionalize innovative thinking throughout the organization.

Innovation and Six Sigma Initiatives

The current body of knowledge for Six Sigma Black Belts does not include innovation. Experience shows that without innovation, breakthrough improvements cannot be realized.

The tools included in the Define, Measure, Analyze, Improve, and Control (DMAIC) methodology allow practitioners to make decisions based on facts or identify causes of existing problems. The Six Sigma practitioner, however, must apply any of the Six Sigma tools creatively for achieving dramatic improvement.

Innovation and DMAIC

In institutionalizing innovation for Six Sigma projects, innovation must become a main tenet of DMAIC. In other words, the project teams must immediately determine to look for an innovative solution in the Define phase. This approach allows the project team to define problems with the expectation for significant improvement innovatively.

The Measure phase allows the team members to understand the process through various performance measurements including simple statistical tools such as mean and standard deviation. Using a more graphical representation of data is sometimes preferable in order to internalize the problem with 'what if' scenarios. In the Analyze phase, root innovative thinking could be in the root cause analysis for identifying potential causes beyond the initial ones. When identifying causes, the principles of TRIZ, the Six Hats of Thinking, and Counter Intuitive Thinking may be used. During the Analyze phase, the objective must be to define the 'total' domain of the problem in terms of its variables, and then innovatively expand the problem domain using innovative thinking.

In the Improve phase, experimenting with a combination of variables with likely significant impact is desirable. To develop an innovative solution, 'go outside the box' and create alternative solutions. 'Going outside the box' means to imagine performance closer to the 'ideal' world, or a totally different approach. The Control phase can help to sustain innovative thinking to continually achieve dramatic improvement of processes and products.

Incorporating Innovation

While preparing to launch a Six Sigma initiative, expect to make a significant improvement in performance based on innovative thinking. Concepts of incremental improvement must be discouraged, because they lead to mediocre solutions and prevent people from realizing the full potential of the initiative.

The leadership must identify and assimilate innovation into a company's values by determining corporate beliefs and tactics and creating an environment for innovation. Leaders must also define innovation in the organizational context and develop a corporate strategy for achieving the innovative success.

Above all else, leaders should establish the expectation and recognition for innovation from employees at all levels. Innovation strategies should include training; communication of expectations and objectives; delineation of the roles of executives, managers and employees; intellectual property management, and commercialization of innovative products or services.

Starting innovation at the personal level, one can look into the following traits practiced by most innovators:

 ➤ A quick system level understanding to speed up the creativity process.

 ➤ Unique and thoughtful ways to overcome obstacles or get around constraints.

 ➤ The ability to optimize a solution while exploiting many constraints.

 ➤ Commitment to change the paradigm.

CHAPTER SEVEN

MAKING SIX SIGMA WORK

Six Sigma is perceived as an expensive initiative with a huge potential for return on investment. However, risks are associated with it. False starts, lack of commitment, and lack of planning may lead to unsatisfactory results. The Six Sigma initiative requires total commitment in order to implement it successfully. Therefore, to minimize risks and improve ROI, Six Sigma should be treated as a process that needs to be implemented in order to realize better, faster and cost-effective performance.

Based on the application of the Theory of Constraints to the Six Sigma process, Table 7.1 summarizes the following action plan for effective implementation of the Six Sigma initiative.

Table 7.1: Action Items for Implementing Six Sigma

Elevated Constraints	Action Plan to Achieve Goals
Leadership's understanding	Understand Drivers, Opportunity, Scorecard, Value proposition
Scorecard	Implement departmental and corporate measurements for accelerating rate of improvement
Beliefs and Culture	Establish corporate beliefs and create performance-driven culture
Planning	Establish goals and plan to realize improvement

Communication	Communicate with shareholders, employees, customers and suppliers
Performance System	Establish employee performance appraisal system for feedback and skills development
Recognition	Inspire people for achieving success through frequent recognition
Basic Training	Provide basic Six Sigma training
Innovation	Establish expectation and process for innovative solutions
Green Belt Training	Provide project-driven Green Belt training as necessary
Motivating Environment	Reward superior performance, and encourage positive and risk-taking behaviors

The Optimized Six Sigma Implementation Plan

SIPOC (Supplier, Input, Process, Output and Customer) is a great tool to identify various players and related information in the Six Sigma theatre of operation. SIPOC utilizes the process steps, the inputs to the process steps and their sources. SIPOC also identifies process outputs and their destination in order to better understand customer input, interface and interests.

SIPOC incorporates optimized process flow for implementing Six Sigma cost effectively. The process steps in the SIPOC tool reflect modifications to reduce cost and improve performance. For example, if a CEO commits to Six Sigma, SIPOC shows what input will be needed in order for commitment to be real. Similarly, planning for Six Sigma includes input such as a prioritized list of projects, executive team training, a strategy for implementing Six Sigma, resources for training and mentoring employees, measurements of success, and an organizational (ownership) chart.

Another modification to the Six Sigma approach is to implement a corporate performance measurement system. An effective scorecard, (e.g., Six Sigma Business Scorecard or Balanced Scorecard), is implemented with inputs such as a corporate performance measurements, departmental measurements, a frequent performance reviews, and periodic communication with stakeholders. A well-implemented scorecard is a prerequisite to sustain the Six Sigma initiative over a longer term. Besides the scorecard, the leadership must sustain the Six Sigma initiative with some exciting changes, energy and activities.

Table 7.2 provides a good framework for understanding and implementing the Six Sigma initiative well in an organization.

Table 7.2: Implementation Process Steps and Inputs

Needs for Six Sigma Initiative	Process Steps
-Leadership education -Drivers for Six Sigma -Market position -Business opportunity analysis -Qualified Resources -Competitive assessment and awareness -Corporate performance	Commit to Six Sigma

-Internally available, enthusiastic individual with strong leadership and moderate statistical skills	Appoint a Six Sigma corporate leader
-Business opportunity analysis	Identify key areas for profitability improvement
-Prioritized list of projects -Executive team training -Strategy for implementing Six Sigma -Resources for training and mentoring -Measurements of success -Organization (Ownership) chart	Planning for Six Sigma
-Corporate performance measurement model (e.g., Six Sigma Business Scorecard or Balanced Scorecard) -Departmental measurements -Performance review process and frequency -Performance communication with stakeholders	Implement performance measurement system for the Six Sigma initiative
-Competitive compensation information -Commitment to reward and recognize excellence -Commitment to communicate consequences of poor performance -A fair and objective performance review system	Establish a Six Sigma performance driven compensation system

-Communication of Corporate vision, values and goals -Statistical thinking training -Six Sigma awareness training -Innovative thinking training -Time management skills training	Conduct basic training for employees
-Projects for improvement -Green Belt training -Experienced Black Belt for mentoring	Conduct project-driven Six Sigma training
-Departmental measurements -Corporate scorecard -Financial results	Verify quantifiable impact on bottom line because of above projects
-Successful completion of projects with significant savings -Innovative solutions -Extraordinary effort and results -Recognition process	Recognize success
-Qualified candidates for Black Belt expertise (Buy or Build) -Project mentors from successful project teams - Lessons learned	Develop internal expertise and resources
-New projects -Project teams -Expanded Six Sigma capability based on needs	Institutionalize Six Sigma methodology
-Scorecard -Continual assessment and renewal	Monitor and sustain improvement

Ref: Gupta, 2004

One of the major challenges is to manage the investment in the Six Sigma initiative. Leadership must make the investment commensurate with the opportunity for profit and growth. The main difference between Six Sigma and other improvement initiatives is that Six Sigma must be utilized for achieving excellence and improving the bottom line.

With a clear understanding of the opportunity, the executive team must establish needs and goals clearly. If a company decides to improve its finances, the goals must be set accordingly. If the objective is to reduce waste by improving processes, goals must be set to achieve an appropriate Six Sigma performance level for various processes.

Due to a possible initial lack of internal qualified resources, corporations are unable to make a firm decision or commit resources to the Six Sigma initiative. Utilizing outside help effectively can reduce initial risks, prevent a false start, and develop a Six Sigma vision and strategic plan. A project leader (sponsor) and a Black Belt are designated to lead the effort, develop a business model, identify growth and profit streams, and list opportunities for improvement. These opportunities are prioritized based on return on investment, and used to define various Six Sigma projects.

Launching Six Sigma

The equation for success is simple. Leadership must inspire so much improvement that the resulting savings are significant enough to share with all stakeholders, including employees. This requires that the leadership team creates an opportunity for such improvement and invests resources in planning this improvement. Company leaders must also investigate opportunities for growth through new innovative products.

Launching a Six Sigma initiative without employee involvement is like driving a car with flat tires. When members of top management implement a new methodology, they deal with mass resistance to change, tell employees to do things in a certain way, train employees in herds, feed employee goals, and assume that employees will produce results in order to keep their jobs.

In order to generate significant savings from a Six Sigma initiative, using statistical techniques is not going to be the key to success; instead, challenging, empowering, supporting, rewarding, and following up with employees will be the inspiration for success. Using a common language, demanding results, and sharing success stories all help to make the Six Sigma initiative successful.

Sustaining Six Sigma

To sustain the Six Sigma initiative, the corporation must create a culture that encourages a passion for excellence, motivates employees for continual aggressive improvement, and engages leadership in listening to employees. In today's knowledge age, where information is being continually produced and performance enhancement is perpetually expected, innovation is the savior. This means "think and do it differently."

Experiments show that thinking requires time. Getting employee ideas on a regular basis requires a process for idea management. Businesses, therefore, must implement an idea management process and drive innovation for continually achieving dramatic improvement. Most importantly, the management must give employees time to think rather than keeping them busy running around.

Sometimes, thinking employees may look like they are not working; however, such a state of affairs must be acceptable as long as the performance indices are moving in the right direction and the business is achieving its objectives. Letting employees have fun is a way to encourage them to think 'outside of the box' and develop innovative solutions for dramatic improvement.

Six Sigma, lean thinking, scorecards, innovation, CMMI, ITIL, ISO 14001, or ISO 9001 must not be seen as separate initiatives. An *integrated* approach to effectively utilize and implement these initiatives must be devised due to limited resources. Lean thinking affects efficiency, Six Sigma influences performance improvement, innovation is designed for new solutions, scorecards are used for driving an economic use of various resources (including these methodologies), and finally, ISO 9001 sustains the use of all these methodologies.

The ISO 9001 system can be used to cultivate process thinking and integrate a right proportion of Six Sigma, lean thinking, innovation and scorecards. In other words, do not take an expert's word for your business; instead develop your own recipe of Six Sigma, lean thinking, innovation and scorecards for your corporation's performance improvement initiative.

Getting Ready to Go

When considering the implementation of Six Sigma, the leadership ponders its benefits and drawbacks and may be concerned about Six Sigma's impact on personal life. Table 7.3 identifies a few issues to clarify in order to commit to Six Sigma.

Table 7.3: Leadership Understanding Assessment

Item #	Six Sigma Consideration	Yes/No
1	Intent of dramatic improvement	
2	Impact on the organization	
3	Resource requirements	
4	Rate of improvement required (>60% /year reduction in waste)	
5	Key tools	
6	Value proposition	
7	Personal benefits	

Besides leadership readiness, one can assess the organizational readiness using Table 7.4.

Table 7.4: Organizational Readiness Assessment

Item #	Readiness Consideration	Yes/No
1	Marginal bottom line performance	
2	Unable to keep up with customer demands	
3	Too many customer complaints	
4	Relatively large quality staff	

5	Limited employee growth or incentives/ recognition	
6	None or insignificant improvement over the past 12 – 36 months	
7	Losing market share or no net revenue growth	

If any of the items in Table 7.4 indicate opportunities for improvement, the Six Sigma initiative can help the organization realize its full potential to produce best-in-class products or services with the highest profit margin.

CONCLUSION

Why pursue Stat Free Six Sigma? Many Six Sigma initiatives are misguided with too much statistics and too little improvement. Six Sigma does sound statistical in nature; in reality, however, it is a strategic initiative with a touch of statistics.

Six Sigma is designed to accelerate improvement using an integrated and comprehensive approach with an extensive tool box consisting of 80% non-statistical tools and only 20% statistical tools. The real improvement comes from a few key tools rather than all of the tools. The following chart demonstrates the role of statistics in process improvement. Practical knowledge consists of extensive process knowledge supported by statistical thinking. The figure on the next page shows that in order to solve problems, we must possess significant process knowledge, and some statistics knowledge, as shown in the Stat Free Six Sigma Domain. Only exceptional circumstances require significant knowledge of the statistics.

The most important aspect of Six Sigma is its ability to channel corporate energy into continually creating value and intellectually engaging employees by challenging them for dramatic improvement. Expecting innovative solutions will lead to innovative employees. Organizations recruit knowledgeable people but are often unable to exploit their knowledge, which is a huge waste with no salvage value.

We believe this book will help readers in implementing a Six Sigma initiative without the fear of statistics, as well as refocusing energies to achieve the intent of Six Sigma, which is a lot of improvement very quickly.

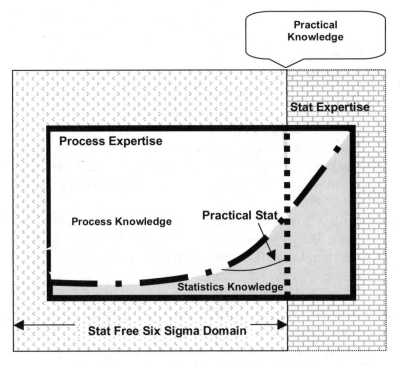

Practical Knowledge for Six Sigma

Bibliography

1. Gupta, Praveen, Six Sigma Business Scorecard: A Comprehensive Corporate Performance Scorecard, McGraw-Hill, NY 2004
2. Gupta, Praveen (2004). The Six Sigma Performance Handbook, McGraw-Hill, NY 2004
3. Gupta, Praveen, Business Innovation in the 21st Century, BookSurge, SC, 2007
4. Harry, M, and Schroeder, R., Six Sigma: The Breakthrough Management Strategy Revolutionizing the World's Top Corporations, Currency and Doubleday, NY, 2000
5. Our Six Sigma Challenge, Motorola, Inc., Issue 3
6. Smith, Bill, The Motorola Story, Motorola, Inc. 1989
7. Therrien, Lois, "The Rival Japan Respects," BusinessWeek, November 1989,
8. Weisz, Bill, "What is Six Sigma: The Video Tape Message," Motorola, Inc. June 1997
9. Wiggenhorn, W. (1990), "Motorola U: When Triaing Becomes an Education," Harvard Business Review July-August 1990

A NOTE FROM THE PUBLISHER

Accelper Consulting has developed four new business improvement methodologies based on our 25 years of experience with corporations of many sizes and industries. The four new methods that we have developed are the following:

1. Simplified Six Sigma Methodology
2. Business Scorecard
3. 4P-Model of Process Excellence
4. Breakthrough Innovation Methodology

If you would like to accelerate rate of improvement, and achieve sustained profitable growth, Accelper Consulting can help you with the following capabilities:

Analyze Your Needs: Experts from Accelper will visit your operations, meet with executives and employees, gather data to understand the real performance issues, and provide a set of recommendations.

Support Your Performance Improvement Initiatives: Accelper offers practical Six Sigma and Innovation training at all levels, and consulting services to support your business objectives.

Answer Your Questions: If you have any question about Six Sigma or innovation, or our approach to performance improvement, please feel free to call us at **1 (800) 680-0700**, or (847) 884-1900, or contact us via email **info@accelper.com**.